Contents

006
PART ONE
Take your first steps
Advice on how to set your marathon goals

020
PART TWO
What do you need?
Choosing the right shoes and kit to wear

040
PART THREE
Starting training
The first steps on the road to running a marathon

060
PART FOUR
Preparing for a run
Warming up, conditioning and stretching

084
PART FIVE
Nutrition explained
How to correctly fuel your training and racing

098
PART SIX
Check the technique
Make your running style as efficient as possible

112
PART SEVEN
Talking training
Getting serious about your running training

124
PART EIGHT
Injury prevention
The lowdown on how to avoid running injuries

138 RACE DAY
The big day's arrived. Race tips, tactics, fuelling and recovery

150 SCHEDULES
12-week schedules for all abilities

The Ultimate Guide to Marathon Running

FOREWORD

By international marathon runner Liz yelling

Liz Yelling is a two-time Olympian (Athens and Beijing) in the marathon and a Commonwealth medalist. She has a marathon personal best of 2hrs 28mins and has competed as a world-class endurance runner in some of the biggest international races. Liz has represented Great Britain at 10 World and European cross-country championships. Although Liz is an elite runner, she is not elitist and understands real running: she coaches runners of all abilities to better performances.

Running a marathon isn't just about lacing up a pair of trainers, turning up on the start line and running 26.2 miles. It's so much more than that. From the moment you decide a marathon is your personal mountain to climb, it's a journey that takes considerable motivation, planning, preparation and effort. The marathon is more than a race. It's an adventure. It's rarely a straightforward trip from entry to finish line and journeys are frequently littered with obstacles, fear, anxiety, disbelief, hope, courage, smiles, grimaces, pain and glory. When I stood on the start line for the Beijing Olympic Games, I'd prepared for the race of my life and was physically and mentally in the best shape I'd ever been.

After leading the field for the first 10 miles, getting tripped up and breaking a rib wasn't in my plan. Just to finish became a real physical and emotional battle, and my ultimate goal.

Whatever your marathon goal, being prepared for the entire journey goes hand in hand with a successful finish. The Ultimate Guide to Marathon Running will help inform, educate and inspire you to complete the necessary training and the race itself. From advice on buying the correct footwear and clothing, to what to eat, why and when, how to run, what running to do and the best things to eat and drink, this guide really is a comprehensive toolkit for everything you need to know to help you achieve your marathon dreams. Many first-time marathon runners experience setbacks along the way, many of these down to inexperience and poor advice. This book provides the ultimate insight into how to prepare brilliantly for your race. It will help to answer your training questions: how long should you run for and when; what happens if you get injured or ill; what is fartlek? It shows you how to plan and progress your running, provides relevant and appropriate training schedules for all abilities, and helps you take all the steps, literally and metaphorically, needed to finish the race with a big smile on your face.

Brace yourself for your marathon adventure. *The Ultimate Guide to Marathon Running* is your training companion from entry through to finish line. Good luck – go for it!

CONTRIBUTORS

Editor Lucas Ellis
Lucas is a runner and journalist (in that order). He's been competing since the age of 11 and has run numerous 10ks, half-marathons and marathons. With a BSc in PE and sports science, he writes about running for some of the UK's leading health and fitness publications.

Chief Contributor Sarah Russell
Sarah has an MSc in sport science and 17 years' experience as a trainer, coach, competitive rower, runner and triathlete. She has run several marathons and regularly writes about running in the UK press.

Contributor Roy Stevenson
Roy wrote about running technique. With a masters degree in coaching and exercise physiology, Roy has competed in New Zealand championships on the track, road and cross country, coaching hundreds of serious and recreational runners in the Seattle area.

Design Andrew Hill

Management
MagBook Publisher Dharmesh Mistry
Digital Production Manager Nicky Baker
Operations Director Robin Ryan
Managing Director of Advertising Julian Lloyd-Evans
Newstrade Director David Barker
Chief Operating Officer Brett Reynolds
Group Finance Director Ian Leggett
Chief Executive James Tye
Chairman Felix Dennis

MAGBOOK

The MagBook brand is a trademark of Dennis Publishing Ltd, 30 Cleveland St, London W1T 4JD. Company registered in England. All material © Dennis Publishing Ltd, licensed by Felden 2011, and may not be reproduced in whole or part without the consent of the publishers.
The Ultimate Guide to Marathon Running
ISBN [ISBN: 1-907779-43-4]

Licensing
To license this product please contact Hannah Heagney on +44 (0) 20 7907 6134 or email hannah_heagney@dennis.co.uk
To syndicate content from this product please contact Anj Dosaj Halai on +44 (0) 20 7907 6132 or email anj_dosaj-halai@dennis.co.uk

Liability
While every care was taken during the production of this MagBook, the publishers cannot be held responsible for the accuracy of the information or any consequence arising from it. Dennis Publishing takes no responsibility for the companies advertising in this MagBook.
The paper used within this MagBook is produced from sustainable fibre, manufactured by mills with a valid chain of custody.
Printed at BGP Bicester

The Ultimate Guide to Marathon Running

RunBreeze

FOCUS ON YOUR GOALS. NOT YOUR FEET.

THE ANTI-BLISTER SOCK £8

Featuring double-layered technology, the two layers rub against each other instead of your foot. This helps to prevent blisters, which means you can run easier, freer, faster.

facebook.com/runbreeze   twitter.com/runbreeze

SAVE 10%* when you purchase any RunBreeze technical sock online today. Visit www.runbreeze.com and enter code marathonguide10 to claim your discount. Plus, free P&P on all orders over £10.

* Save 10% off of your first order only redeemable at www.runbreeze.com.
** Free postage and packaging over £10 on all UK mainland orders only. International postage fees apply, see website for details. RunBreeze reserve the right to change or withdraw this offer at any time. Offer ends 1st September 2012.

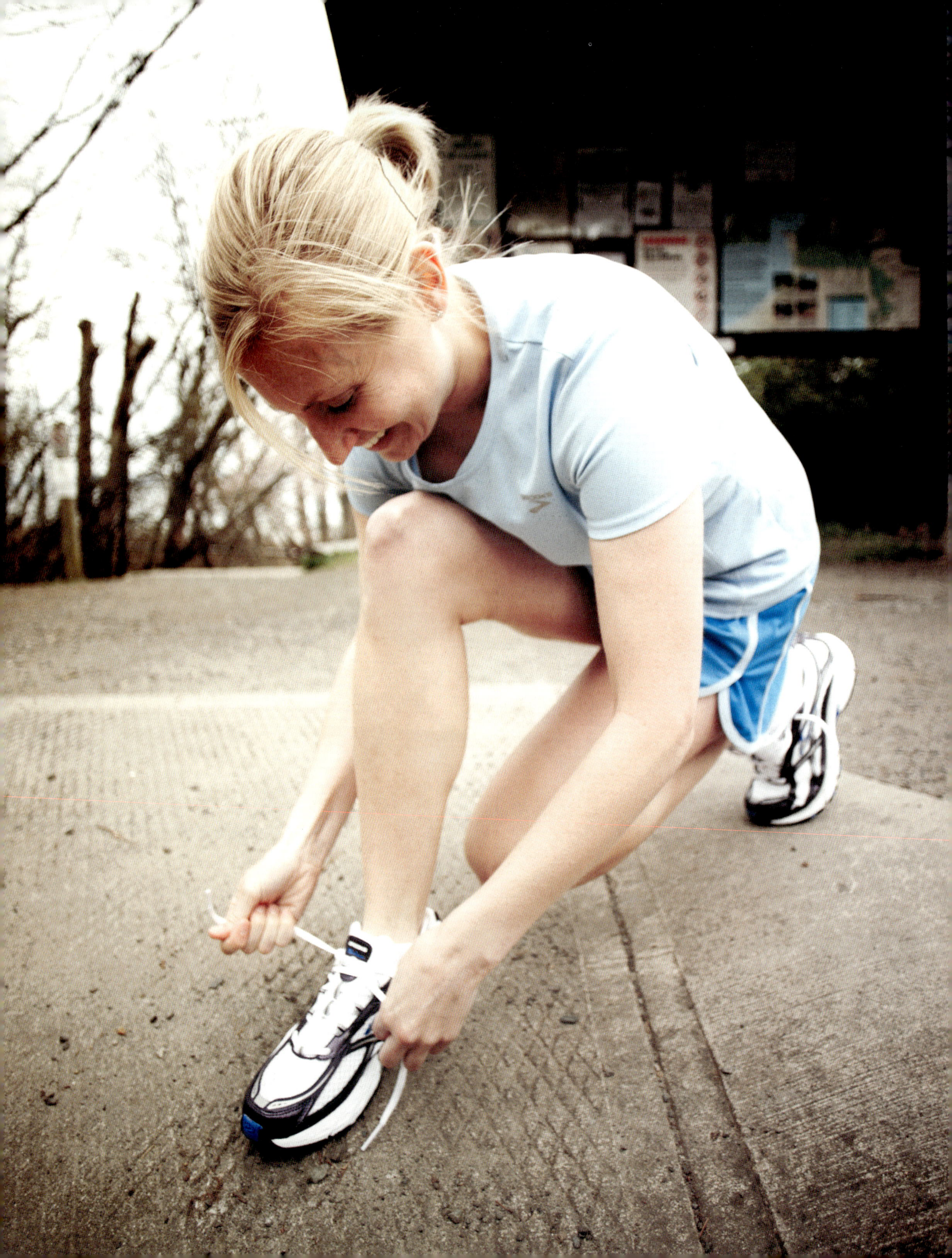

Part one

TAKING THE FIRST STEPS

Marathon running's allure has grown inexorably in the past 20 years. Whereas, in the early 1980s, there were only a handful of big city races, now you could run a marathon every weekend – providing you were willing to travel a bit! Why the classic 26.2-mile distance should have captured people's imaginations quite as much as it has is something of a mystery, particularly to people who have never run one. But for anyone crossing the marathon finish line for the first time, it's that very action that defines the whole marathon experience. Running a marathon is undoubtedly an emotional experience: it unites people in a sense of real achievement; it is a true physical test; and it's something that means so much to so many. It's difficult to capture all of these feelings in a book, but, hopefully, by the time you finish reading the advice, tips, hints and information in this publication, you'll have gained an appreciation of just what running a marathon really means.

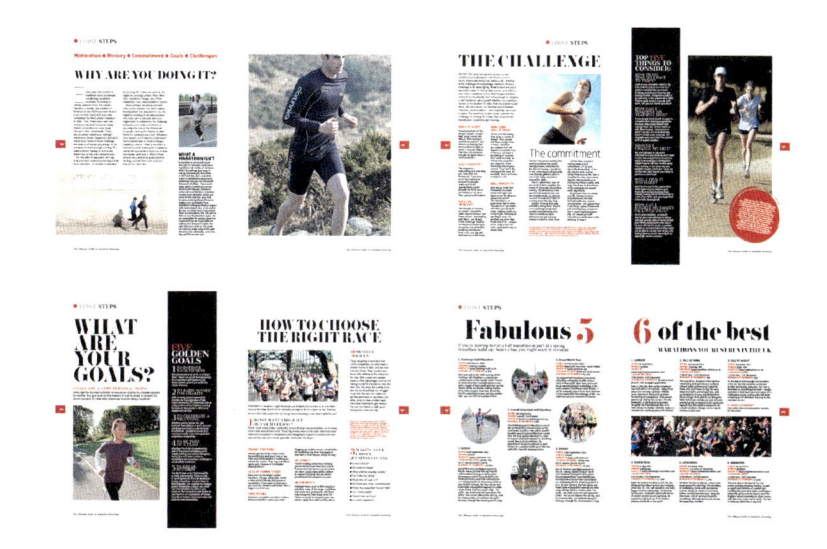

007

WE ARE DIFFERENT, IN ESSENCE, FROM OTHER MEN. IF YOU WANT TO WIN SOMETHING, RUN 100 METRES. IF YOU WANT TO EXPERIENCE SOMETHING, RUN A MARATHON **EMIL ZATOPEK**

The Ultimate Guide to Marathon Running

● FIRST STEPS

The Ultimate Guide to Marathon Running

WHAT DOES THE MARATHON MEAN TO ME?

I'D NEVER wanted to run a marathon. As a former middle-distance runner, the thought of running 26.2 miles - the classic marathon distance - frightened, appalled and terrified me in equal measure. But, like many of you out there preparing for your first marathon, I had a 'eureka' moment when I decided that I absolutely had to run a marathon, even if it was the last thing I ever did. That moment came when I went to watch the 2007 Flora London Marathon. As a member of the press, I was lucky enough to gain access to otherwise-prohibited areas and experience the marathon 'up close and personal'. It was a fantastic experience and one that I, too, wanted to be a part of. Until that point, although I was - and still am - a keen runner, my marathon experience had been limited to a comfy armchair and TV coverage every time the London Marathon rolled around. That all changed when I saw the thousands of runners cheered on by spectators lining the streets: it truly is a breathtaking sight. And now I'm hooked.

About this book

If you're reading this book, you've already taken the first step towards running a marathon. Equally, you might be looking for advice and inspiration to improve your best. The content here is about as comprehensive a guide to running a marathon as you'll get. It's practical and should take you step-by-step through some of the key decisions that you'll need to make in your marathon training. While it's slanted towards beginners and first-timers, it's packed full of advice that even experienced runners will benefit from. You'll find helpful tips on everything from buying the right running shoes to how to motivate yourself come race day; you'll also be given instruction in to how to form your own training plans as well as more prescriptive schedules for a variety of marathon speeds.

To put it simply: if it's not in this book, then it's probably not worth knowing.

The Ultimate Guide to Marathon Running

● **FIRST STEPS**

Motivation ● **History** ● **Commitment** ● **Goals** ● **Challenges**

WHY ARE YOU DOING IT?

Every year, the number of marathon races and people completing marathons increases. According to official statistics from the London Marathon website, the number of finishers in the 2008 race was 34,420, a far cry from the 6,500 or so who completed the first London Marathon in 1981. Then, there were very few marathons around the world: today, there's a marathon in every major city and a few more beside. There are mountain marathons, midnight marathons, desert marathons and arctic marathons. Some of these challenge the realms of human physiology to the extreme: it's hard enough running 26.2 miles without having to do it in the desert sun or sub-zero temperatures.

For the sake of argument, let's say that you have entered something a little more standard – or at least as standard as running 26.2 miles can ever be. You might be running London, Paris, New York, Boston or Chicago, one of the marathons that come steeped in history.

You'll probably be asking yourself why you've entered. For some reason, the marathon has appealed to you. You might be wanting to emulate a friend who took part in one last year; you might want to experience the challenge and push your body to its limits; or you might be one of the thousands of people running for charity to raise funds for someone you know. Whatever your reason, you'll need to understand the fundamentals of what running a marathon means – what a marathon is (and isn't); what training for a marathon can do for you; what it costs you in time and money (and how it affects those around you); and what goals you'll be setting yourself from now until you step on the start line.

WHAT A MARATHON ISN'T

A marathon is not a stroll round the park; it's not even a long run. A marathon is 26.2 miles of continual effort that will sap your body of energy and leave you exhausted at the finish line. But a marathon is also an exhilarating experience, something that you can share with thousands of others. There aren't many sports in which you can toe the line with Olympic champions and world record holders: marathon running is not exclusive. When you stand on the start line, you could be doing so alongside world record holders such as Britain's Paula Radcliffe or Ethiopian distance legend Haile Gebrselassie. But, at the end of the day, no matter how many people there are around you, the only person that can run the marathon is you. You are responsible for getting round the course and you are responsible for making sure that you've taken the right measures to do so. This book can help you make many of the right decisions, but, ultimately, come race day, you'll be on your own.

The Ultimate Guide to Marathon Running

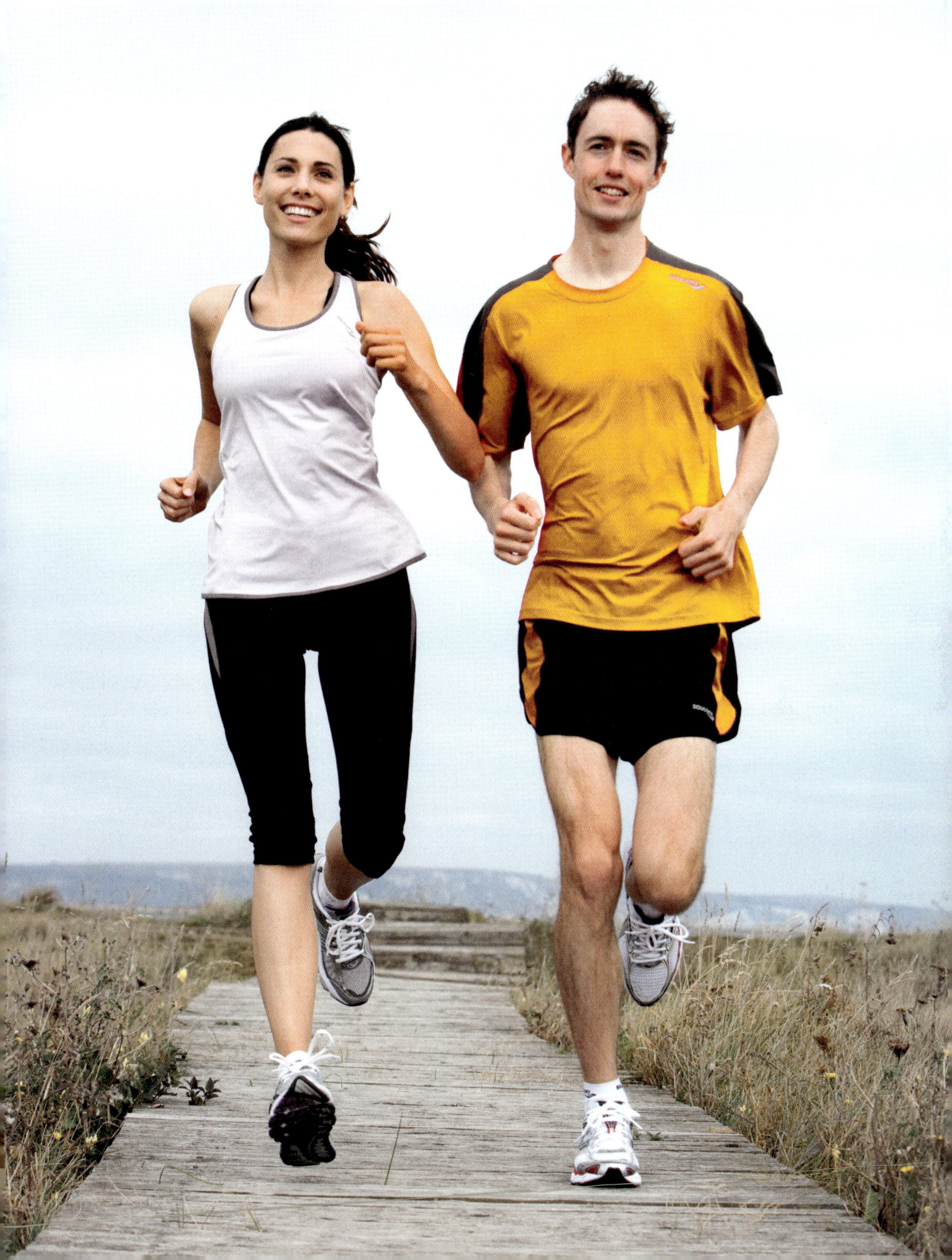

● FIRST **STEPS**

The first marathon

THERE HAD to be somebody to blame for putting millions of people through the pain of running a marathon. For the first evidence, you need to rewind to 500BC and Pheidippides, a Greek soldier, who, legend has it, ran with the news of a battle from the plains of Marathon to the City of Athens, which was just under 25 miles away. He finished the distance, managed to cough out the word 'niki' (victory), collapsed and promptly died – not a great advert for running a marathon.

At the first modern Olympics in 1896, officials held a marathon to commemorate Pheidippides' run. The distance was 24.85 miles and was won by Greek Spiridon Louis in just under 3 hours. It wasn't until 1908, with the London Olympics, that the modern distance of 26.2 miles came into being. Organisers wanted to start the race at Windsor Castle and end it at the White City stadium, 26 miles away. They then added 0.2 miles so that the race could finish right in front of the royal family – and so the official distance of the marathon was changed from 24.85 to 26.2 miles. So you now know who to blame if you're suffering in the last mile.

You don't run 26 miles at five minutes a mile on good looks and a secret recipe
Frank Shorter

The Ultimate Guide to Marathon Running

Who are you training with today?

SHAPE UP WITH L-CARNITINE LIQUID

AVAILABLE IN INDEPENDENT HEALTH FOOD STORES

SOLGAR VITAMIN AND HERB
essentials for life's journey
www.solgar.com/uk

● FIRST STEPS

THE CHALLENGE

NO MATTER what standard of runner you are, whether you're aiming for sub 3 hours or sub 5 hours, there's one thing that unites us all - and that is the challenge of completing a marathon. It's not a challenge to be taken lightly. Break it down and you'll see what I mean. If the furthest you've run is 10k in a race, then a marathon is four times longer (and then some); if you've already been lucky enough to complete a half marathon, ask yourself whether you could have carried on for another 13 miles: I bet the answer would be no. But don't worry. By the time you've finished this book, you'll be able to - and, hopefully, have room to spare. The point here is don't under-estimate the challenge of running 26.2 miles. Even experienced marathoners sometimes get it wrong.

DOES IT HURT?
Everyone's heard of the phrase 'no pain, no gain'. Well, every runner will tell you that running is sometimes painful - and there's no denying that the marathon is right up there in the pain stakes. The trick is to minimise the pain by laying down a firm foundation.

WILL I MAKE IT?
The answer is a resounding 'yes' providing you have done the homework. If you have put in the training for your particular goal, eaten and drunk appropriately, paced yourself correctly and if you think you can do it, then, yes, you will make it.

WILL I BE NERVOUS?
The thought of running 26.2 miles is bound to make anyone nervous. But those nerves - and dealing with them - are all part of the challenge. Positive nervousness is what gets you going: the adrenaline pumping around your body come race day will help fuel you to the finish.

HOW LONG WILL IT TAKE?
That's a bit like asking 'how long is a piece of string?'. Most people will have a target time in mind - whether you achieve that will depend on a whole host of factors, not least a sprinkling of 'runner's luck' come race day. No matter how prepared you might be, there are things beyond your control. If you don't like running in the heat, for example, then you'll have to hope for rain.

WILL I ENJOY IT?
Why do you think that thousands of people come back again and again to run the distance around the world? The marathon is an experience like no other. Thousands of spectators will cheer you along the route, helping propel you to the finish. Most people say they'll never run another one when they finish their first - and yet, often, they're back for more, sometimes only six weeks later.

The commitment

The fact that you're reading this book is evidence that you've already at least committed to the idea of running a marathon. In fact, most of you will probably have already gained a place in one of the many marathons around the globe.

This is a great start. Now all you need to do is complete the weeks of physically demanding training, the abstinence from alcohol and sweet treats, and the stressful build-up, and put yourself through 26.2 miles of running come race day. Easy.

And yet, if it was that easy, we'd all be doing them, there'd be no challenge and people wouldn't give admiring (and often incredulous) looks whenever you get out your finisher's medal to show them.

Let's be clear: marathon training takes a lot of commitment. It's not just physically demanding - it can also place a strain on your family life and social life. Even a schedule for a five-hour runner requires that you build up to training four times a week, with long runs of two to three hours at the weekends and several week-day efforts.

But you don't have to change your life. The best training programmes are the ones that work with your current circumstances - not against them. If you fancy a glass of wine with your evening meal, and you've put in a good training session, why not reward yourself? Everything in moderation is the best way to view it.

Decide what your marathon goal is and stick to it. It may be that simply completing the race is your goal, or you may have a particular time in mind or sum that you want to raise for charity. We all have goals that ARE personal to us — don't get distracted by what anyone else is doing. Stick to your goal and let that guide your marathon journey.

The Ultimate Guide to Marathon Running

TOP FIVE THINGS TO CONSIDER:

HOW MUCH TIME DO I HAVE TO TRAIN?
Look at your schedule: when is the best time for you to run that isn't going to compromise your work or those around you? If you've got young children, it might be easier to go out early at the weekends or after they've gone to bed. If you do shift work, can you run before you start?

HOW CAN I MAXIMISE MY TRAINING TIME?
Some people think they'll struggle to complete their training programme because they simply haven't got enough time. But, where there's a will, there's a way. Can you run to work? Can you run at work during lunch? I know many a teacher, for example, who uses their free period to fit in a quick session.

SHOULD I CHANGE MY DIET?
No, you just need to pay more attention to it: you certainly don't need to start downing platefuls of pasta in order to increase your carbohydrate intake if you're still four months away from race day. In the same way you wouldn't expect a Formula 1 car to run on four star, don't expect your body to perform on junk food.

WILL I FIND IT TOO HARD?
Not if you've put in the preparation that's right for your desired goal. If you fly in on race morning from holiday, having run no further than to catch a bus, then, yes, you might find it too hard. Be prepared.

HOW CAN I INVOLVE MY FAMILY OR LOVED ONES?
Don't run in isolation. Let people around you know what you're doing. Get your partner, kids or friend to hold your drinks bottle during the race or be your 'official' kit carrier. A problem shared is a problem halved: they might not be able to run the race for you, but having them on board, mentally if not physically, can be a comfort.

Like chocolate? Why not try substituting your current favourite for a high-percentage cocoa brand? The health benefits come from chocolate's cocoa content not from its dairy content. Research has shown that the cocoa in chocolate is a rich source of minerals, in particular, magnesium, potassium and copper. These nutrients have a variety of roles in the body, especially critical for athletes, including energy production, muscle contraction and blood circulation. But always try TO opt for brands that have 50% cocoa content or MORE.

015

The Ultimate Guide to Marathon Running

● FIRST STEPS

WHAT ARE YOUR GOALS?

GOALS ARE A VERY PERSONAL THING: what might be the main motivator for one person could be the complete opposite for another. Your goal could be time-based or it could be simply to complete the race in one piece. So what other reasons are there for doing a marathon?

FIVE GOLDEN GOALS

1 TO IMPROVE YOUR FITNESS
Everybody wants to be fit, or at least fitter. There's no doubt that preparing for a marathon will improve your fitness levels, even if you walk the whole distance.

2 TO RAISE MONEY FOR CHARITY
With so many places reserved for charities by the organisers of the major marathons, it's inevitable that as many as 85% of the field are running for some of the country's 1800 or so registered charities.

3 TO CELEBRATE A MILESTONE
Whether you've turned 40, got married, had children or got a new job, running a marathon is a perfect way to celebrate - providing you do your training to make it the unforgettable experience it should be.

4 TO BE PART OF A TEAM
Whether it's at the Championship end of the race or whether you're simply joining your work colleagues, being part of a team united in completing the marathon challenge is an excellent motivator.

5 TO BREAK RECORDS
You don't have to be Paula Radcliffe or Haile Gebrselassie: there are lots of running records that can be broken during a marathon - you just have to think laterally. You could be the fastest person dressed as a clown, you could 'run' the marathon on stilts or you could run the race with a milk bottle on your head or run backwards. All these records are broken more times than the world records themselves.

The Ultimate Guide to Marathon Running

HOW TO CHOOSE THE RIGHT RACE

CHOOSING A marathon might be simple, particularly if you want to do one that's on your doorstep. But if you're not lucky enough to live in a town or city that has its own 26.2-mile event, how do you go about choosing a race that's right for you?

1 DO YOU WANT A BIG RACE OR A SMALLER ONE?

Pretty much every major capital city around Europe has a marathon, as do many other cities around the world. These big events are run like well-oiled machines: there are thousands of competitors and background support to make sure your run, and the race as a whole, goes like clockwork. You'll get:

DRINKS STATIONS
Usually sponsored by a large brand, these will be located every one or two miles and will be helpful in fuelling you around the course. They may even stock sports gels, bananas or (strangely) baked potatoes!

LOTS OF COMPETITORS
Races such as the Virgin London Marathon, Chicago, Rotterdam, Berlin or Paris attract literally thousands of competitors. If you want to share your pain with like-minded individuals, then a bigger race is for you.

SPECTATORS
Someone once said a marathon is about 80% mental effort. When you start flagging around the course, what better lift could there be than thousands of spectators cheering you along the way?

ACCURACY
There's nothing worse than thinking you've clocked a personal best only to find out that the course was 50 metres too short. Larger races will be ratified by a governing body and are almost guaranteed to be pinpoint accurate.

PASTA PARTY
Although these tend to differ largely in standard, many of the larger marathons have a pre-race pasta party, which you may or may not have to pay extra for. These are great for swapping pre-race stories, injury fears and running advice.

2 SMALLER RACES

These are going to have less than 2,000 competitors, are often held in smaller towns or cities, and are more intimate affairs. They usually have fewer elite athletes at the sharp end, but may offer a more picturesque route or other advantages, such as not having to wait 15 minutes to cross the start line. The entry fee is likely to be less and you'll probably not struggle to get into the race. You might not get the same level of spectators, but, often, even in these smaller races, the whole community gets behind the race and there's a really good atmosphere come race day.

If you want a pasta party that really delivers, check out Jamaica's Reggae Marathon, usually held in the first week of December. Hotels along the Negril tourist strip try to outdo each other with fantastic spreads. The food is excellent, it's free to competitors and there's plenty of it, all accompanied by some traditional reggae music.

3 MAKING YOUR CHOICE. QUESTIONS TO ASK:

- Is cost a factor?
- Do I want to travel?
- What will the weather be like?
- Can I take my family?
- What time of year is it?
- Do I have any other commitments?
- What's the course like? Terrain? Hills?
- Can I enter easily?
- Does it have an Expo?
- Is it well-organised?

The Ultimate Guide to Marathon Running

FIRST STEPS

Fabulous 5

If you're looking to run a half marathon as part of a spring marathon build-up, here's a few you might want to consider

1. Hastings Half Marathon
WHEN: 25th March
WHERE: Hastings, Sussex
WEBSITE: www.hastings-half.co.uk
NUMBER OF RUNNERS: 4,000

Next year will be the 28th running of the Hastings Half Marathon, a popular pre-London event on the Sussex coast. There's no doubt that this is a challenging course, with a couple of long uphill sections and the chance of the sea breeze making the last three miles tougher than they should be. But it's a great course and, get the weather right, you can still run a personal best.

2. Aviemore
WHEN: 16th October
WHERE: Cairngorms National Park, Scotland
WEBSITE: www.aviemorehalfmarathon.org
COURSE RECORDS: 1:24.24 Women 1:09.19 Men
NUMBER OF RUNNERS: 900

Taking place in the Cairngorms in the Scottish Highlands, this is probably the most beautiful half marathon in the UK. Raising money for the Speyside Trust, the event only started in 2006, but has fast grown in popularity attracting nearly 1,000 runners in 2009. The route passes through the Glenmore Forest and past Loch Morlich with the Cairngorm Mountains setting a spectacular backdrop. Taking place on a nice mix of tarmac, forest trails and paths, it's a deceptively quick route with quite possibly the most stunning scenery you could ever wish for.

3. Llanelli Waterside Half Marathon
WHEN: 4th March
WHERE: Llanelli, South Wales
WEBSITE: www.humanbeingactive.org
NUMBER OF RUNNERS: 1300

This challenging event takes place in one of the most beautiful and scenic areas of the south Wales coastline. Held within Llanelli's beautiful award winning Millennium Coastal Park, this truly spectacular event is a must for anyone wanting to take part in something special. Now in its seventh year, the popularity of the event continues to build. Perfect for a marathon build-up, it's flat, fast and traffic-free with amazing scenery.

4. Great North Run
WHEN: 18 September
WHERE: Newcastle Upon Tyne - South Shields
WEBSITE: www.greatrun.org
COURSE RECORDS: 59:05 men, 65:40 women
NUMBER OF RUNNERS: 54,000

The biggest Half Marathon in the World, attracting a whopping 54,000 runners, starts in Newcastle Upon Tyne, and winds it way over the famous Tyne Bridge to the coast, where it finishes at South Shields. It can be a speedy course if you don't get stuck in the crowds. With live coverage on BBC, you might just get your moment of fame too.

5. Bristol
WHEN: 11th September
WHERE: Bristol
WEBSITE: www.runbristol.com
COURSE RECORDS: 60:03 Men 66:47 women (world record)
NUMBER OF RUNNERS: 16,000

One of the most prestigious events in the UK, having hosted the IAAF World Half Marathon Champs in 2001 where thousands watched Paula Radcliffe set the World Record and Haile Gebrselassie run a blistering 60:03. Attracting a field of over 16,000 runners, the fast course and impeccable organisation appeals to a wide range of elite and fun runners alike. The scenic, sea-level route isn't just about PBs either - the course takes in the old city, past the Harbourside, out and back along the Portway, through the stunning Avon Gorge,

The Ultimate Guide to Marathon Running

6 of the best

MARATHONS YOU MUST RUN IN THE UK

1. LONDON
WHEN: 17 April
WHERE: London
WEBSITE: www.virginlondonmarathon.com
COURSE RECORDS:
2:05:10 men, 2:15:25 women
NUMBER OF RUNNERS: 36,549 in 2010 (from 51,000 accepted applicants)

Back in 1981 the first London Marathon was held with 7,747 runners. Today it has grown into not only a premier athletic event, but one of the world's greatest fundraising extravaganzas. Many people want to say they've run London - for the landmarks, to participate in an event alongside the international elite, or to raise money for charity. However, expect a crowded race and long queues for the loo!

2. ISLE OF MAN
WHEN: 14 August
WHERE: Ramsey, IOM
WEBSITE: www.marathon.iomvac.co.uk
COURSE RECORDS:
2:30:07 men, 3:08:28 women
NUMBER OF RUNENRS: 300

This marathon, situated on the mystical island lying midway between Scotland, Ireland, Wales and England, is ideal for those who aren't keen on big city races. Expect an idyllic and tranquil race, with an abundance of pure, unpolluted air to fill your lungs. To be able to run alongside fields full of rare orchids and seas rich with wrecks sounds as magical as the myths and legends that this island is steeped in. It's a small marathon, though, so you may be running on your own.

3. ISLE OF WIGHT
WHEN: 9 October
WHERE: Ryde, IOW
WEBSITE: www.rydeharriers.co.uk
COURSE RECORDS:
2.22.02 men, 2.52.56 women
NUMBER OF RUNNERS: 500

As the oldest continuously held marathon in the UK, the IOW marathon celebrates its 56th anniversary next year. The race is described as undulating (translate = tough) and takes in both town and rural roads. It's a challenging course; so if you like hills (with a total ascent of 1505 feet) this may be the marathon for you.

IS THERE A DOWNSIDE?
More often than not the weather is warm for this event.

4. EDINBURGH
WHEN: 22 May
WHERE: Edinburgh
WEBSITE: www.edinburgh-marathon.com
COURSE RECORDS:
2:15:26 men, 2:33:36 women
NUMBER OF RUNNERS: 17,000

Rated the fastest marathon in the UK, the Edinburgh Marathon Festival also includes a junior race, 5k, 10k, half marathon and hairy haggis marathon team relay - something for everyone. Scotland's capital will ensure all runners receive a warm welcome, its popularity making it one of the fastest growing marathons in the world.

5. LOCH NESS
WHEN: 2 October
WHERE: Loch Ness, nr Inverness
WEBSITE: www.lochnessmarathon.com
COURSE RECORDS:
2:20:13 men, 2:46:39 women
NUMBER OF RUNNERS: 1,200

Whether it's clear or stormy, expect to be piped across the start-line, then to follow an undulating course with spectacular scenery along the shores of Loch Ness before running into Inverness, along the River Ness. One of our most beautiful marathons, although don't expect to see the legendary monster!

6. BRIGHTON
WHEN: 10 April
WHERE: Brighton
WEBSITE: www.brightonmarathon.co.uk
COURSE RECORDS:
2:19:05 men, 3:05:20 women
NUMBER OF RUNNERS: 15,000

The race takes in the best of the city centre, including Brighton Pavilion, as well as significant stretches of coastal road, including the panoramic views you'd expect where the glorious South Downs meet the English Channel. Generally it's a fast course, with the entire route free of traffic. The last 15 miles are either flat or downhill.

The Ultimate Guide to Marathon Running

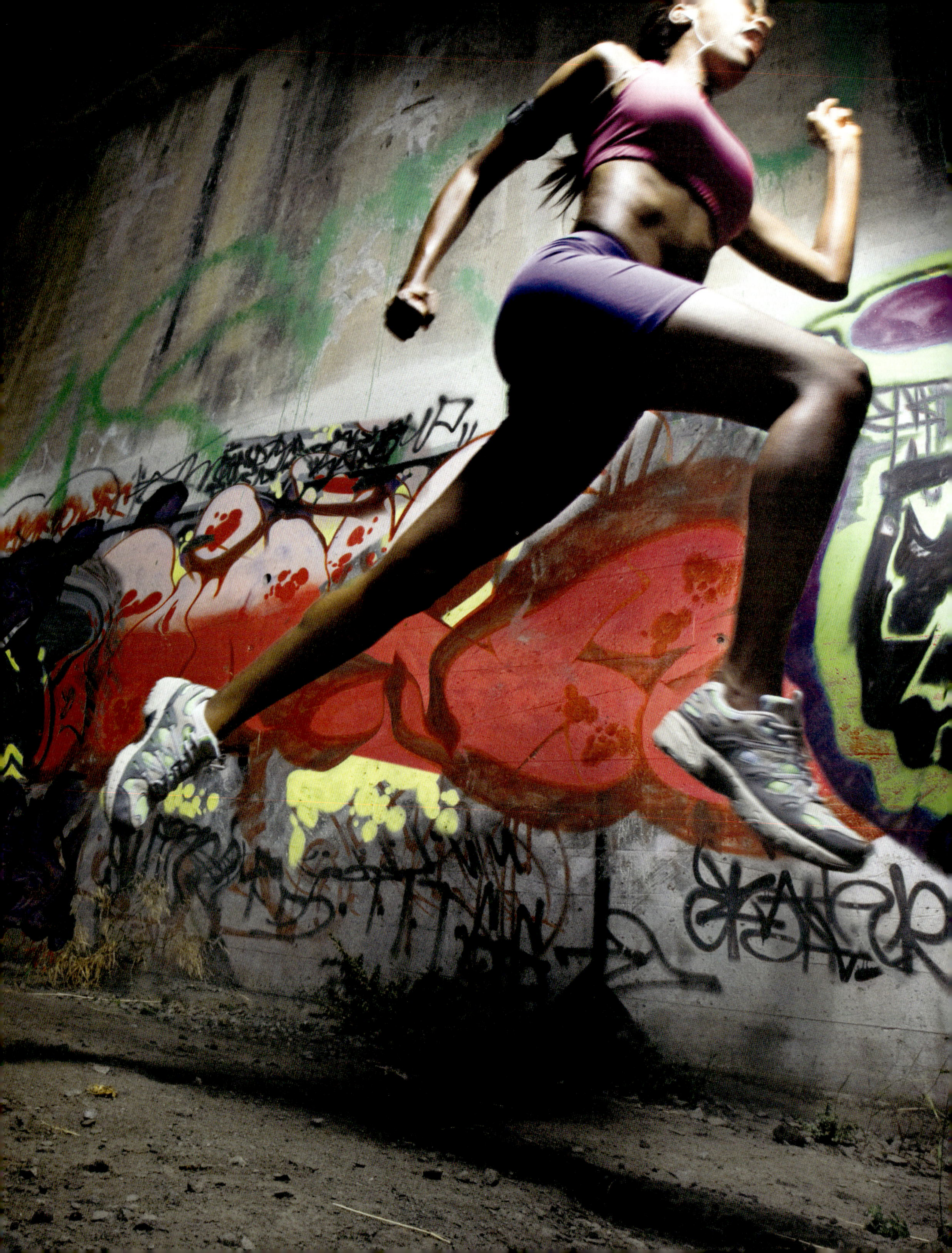

Part two

ESSENTIAL KIT GUIDE

No book on marathon running would be complete without a chapter on what to wear. But this isn't about fashion, it's about finding the shoes and kit that are right for you, and that will make your whole marathon experience one to remember. Pity the runner who wears the wrong shoes over 26.2 miles!

Your shoes and kit are ultimately down to personal preference, but, in this chapter, we lay down some basic rules for choosing the right running shoes and what you'll need to wear if you're preparing to run a marathon, no matter what weather conditions or temperatures you find yourself training in. You'll learn the difference between pronation and supination, the characteristics of various shoe categories and which clothing fabrics work best in what conditions. It's a complete guide to choosing your marathon kit!

YOUR CHOICE OF RUNNING SHOE CAN MAKE THE DIFFERENCE BETWEEN HAVING A GOOD OR BAD EXPERIENCE AND WHETHER OR NOT YOU STAY HEALTHY — OR GET INJURED

The Ultimate Guide to Marathon Running

● ESSENTIAL **KIT**

Shoe choice ● Off-road ● Kit ● Compression ● Peripherals

WHAT TO WEAR

The beauty of running is that, no matter what distance you're attempting, it's about the least complicated sport you can get. We can all run - we might not all be able to run fast or for long, but we can all do something that approximates to a running action. And, if you can do that, you're on your way!

However, before you start a training programme, it's important to buy the right running kit (clothing, shoes and peripherals) so that you don't feel uncomfortable when you start to rack up the mileage - particularly in your marathon training.

Your first consideration should always be your shoes. With so many different brands and varieties available, it's easy to be blinded by science. In this chapter, we outline some of the things to look for when buying a pair of running shoes. Remember, you've got 26.2 miles to run: making the wrong choice, buying ill-fitting shoes or not listening to advice won't just cost you lost time in a marathon, it could mean the difference between running injury-free - or not being able to run at all.

While your choice of running clothing might not be quite as critical, things have moved on a long way since the days of only cotton T-shirts being available. Today's running clothing is made from some of the most advanced fabrics known to man. There are jackets made of fabrics that are impervious to water, but still let the body breathe; there are tops that are so lightweight they can be folded into a trouser pocket; and there are even tops with air chambers that can be inflated when the temperature drops. To put it bluntly, if you can think of an application, then there's probably a piece of running clothing that will do the job.

While you can 'make do' with any clothing that feels comfortable, you won't want the uncomfortable feeling of a water-logged T-shirt weighing you down or some old shorts chafing the skin between your legs - particularly if you're on a long training run or during the marathon event itself.

Buying the right kit can make your marathon journey just that bit more bearable - and believe me when I say you'll want all the help you can get!

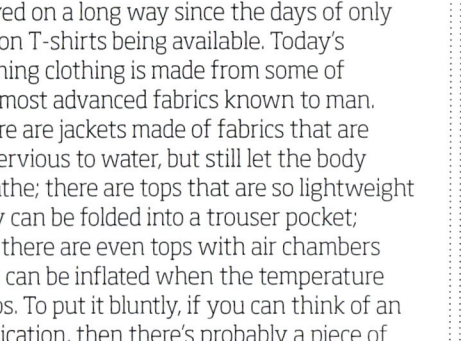

THINGS TO THINK ABOUT
Some of the factors that you should consider when buying clothing are:
- its ability to move freely with your body.
- the fabric's wicking ability.
- how lightweight it is.
- whether the waterproof clothing remains waterproof during the most miserable weather.
- style - what does it look like? Don't base all your decisions on aesthetics, but, equally, you want to look and feel good.

WHAT YOU NEED (ESSENTIAL):
- Running shoes
- Socks
- Windproof/waterproof jacket (preferably breathable)
- Long-sleeved top (especially for winter)
- T-shirt
- Shorts (with inner brief - men)
- Sports bra (women)

WHAT YOU NEED (DESIRABLE):
- Breathable jacket
- Running tights
- Hat/gloves
- Thermal top (breathable and worn next to skin)

WHAT YOU NEED (OPTIONAL):
- Compression clothing
- Sunglasses

The Ultimate Guide to Marathon Running

CHOOSING YOUR SHOES

Running shoes are, without a doubt, the most important piece of kit that any runner - whether they are just taking their first steps into the sport or whether they are seasoned athletes - can buy.

Your choice of running shoes can make the difference between having a good or bad experience, running in comfort or pain and, most importantly, whether you stay healthy or get injured.

Shoe technology has improved dramatically during my running career: nowadays, there are shoes for every foot type, every running style and every terrain. There are women-specific shoes, shoes for pushing the pace - there are even shoes specific to treadmill running.

Every major running brand has a wide range of shoes that cater for runners of all shapes and sizes: all you need to do is make sure you buy the right ones for you.

Running shoes tend to be the most expensive part of a runner's outfit, so it's important that you make the right decision about your footwear. However, my first rule would be 'don't buy on price alone'.

If you opt for the cheapest pair, regardless of fit, you will not necessarily be getting the right shoe for you; equally, buying the most expensive pair will see you rewarded with a host of technologies that may or may not be suitable for your feet - or your running style.

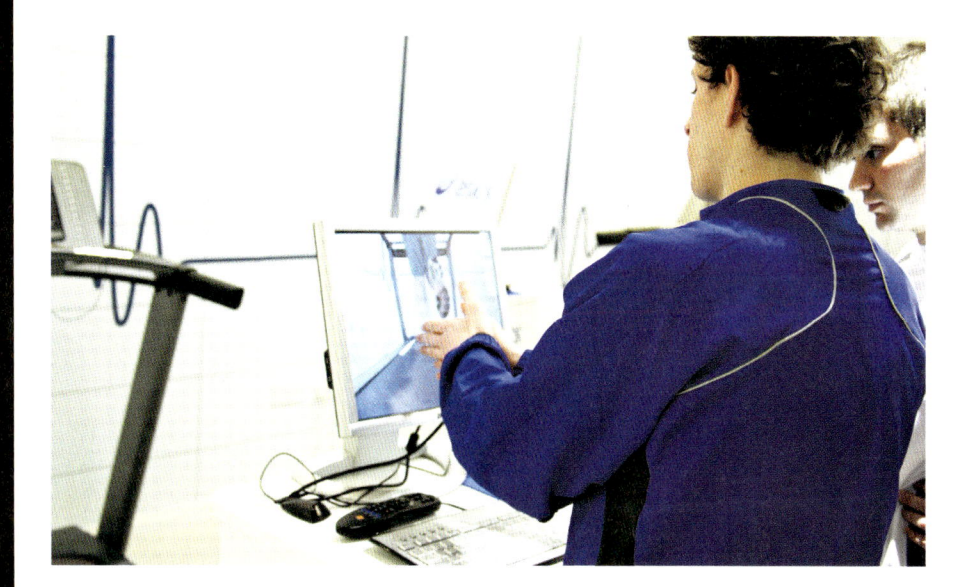

First steps

THE FIRST thing you should do is visit a specialist running retailer who is able to impart independent and knowledgeable advice. Good running-store staff will, most likely, ask you whether you've run before, how many miles you plan to do and what type of surface you'll be running on. The answers to such questions can help them to steer you in the right direction.

Many of these retailers may also offer some form of 'running analysis', whereby your style is analysed using a treadmill, a camera and computer. From this, they'll be able to tell what sort of runner you are and what sort of shoe you will need.

Running shoes fall into a number of categories designed for different runner types. Descriptors such as 'motion control', 'support', 'guidance' and 'neutral' all relate to shoe types and feature technologies that complement the runner's style - or gait - or correct any imbalances.

You'll probably hear the term 'pronation' bandied around in any conversation about buying running shoes. Pronation is the rolling of the foot from heel to toe through the foot strike. Pronation, in itself, is not a bad thing because it helps your feet and legs absorb shock. However, excessive pronation - rolling in too much - can cause increased injury risks. That's called over-pronation, and the answer to it is finding a shoe with good motion control or guidance properties.

A much less frequent problem is supination. Runners who do this tend to have inflexible feet (and, often, high arches, too) and, when they land, their feet don't make much of a rolling-in motion. The result is a lot of pounding force and they need a shoe with plenty of cushioning, or support, to absorb the shock.

Once you've established what type of shoe you'll need, it comes down to choosing a brand. You may have a personal favourite, but it's worth keeping an open mind about your shoe choice. Many runners experiment with different brands and models until they find just the right fit, feel and functionality. Ultimately, a proper fit is the most important step in finding the right running shoe. A shoe that fits will be snug, but not too tight.

Once you've found running shoes that feel right, walk/jog/run in them as much as you can. Some stores have a treadmill, others allow a run around the car park and some don't let you do anything other than bounce up and down. But it's important that you feel the shoes in action.

The Ultimate Guide to Marathon Running

● ESSENTIAL KIT

HOW MUCH SHOULD YOU EXPECT TO PAY?

Few people need the most expensive shoes on the market. The more efficient a runner you are, the less likely you will be to need all the support and guidance features of the top-end shoes.

At the top end of the scale, shoes are likely to be in the £100-£125 bracket; a mid-price shoe will be £65-90; and the cheapest, under £60. Of course, if you don't necessarily want this season's colours, and are happy to be wearing last year's model, there are a number of retailers who sell discounted versions of what is, essentially, the same shoe.

Manufacturers tend to tweak their shoe ranges twice a year. It's a bit like buying a car - if you want the latest model, you'll pay the top price; if you're happy to go for something that's been available for longer, you could get a bargain.

HOW OFTEN SHOULD YOU CHANGE YOUR SHOES?

It depends on the brand, but the rule of thumb is to change your shoes at least every 400 or 500 miles. This means that, if you're running 50 miles a week, you need to change your shoes at least every 10 weeks; run more miles than that and you'll need a new pair sooner.

When you begin your marathon training, you'll probably be completing mileage that you've never done previously - no matter what your race goal. Running shoes were not meant to last indefinitely: not only do the technologies have a finite life, but exposure to the elements (mud, water, snow) during a typical English winter all take their toll.

Many people choose to 'rotate' their shoes with another pair i.e. have one pair for off-road running and one for road running. This should extend the life cycles of each pair.

Your shoes might not look worn out, but often the damage done to them is on the inside, where it's not possible to see: they won't be able to provide the same levels of support, cushioning or guidance. Not replacing aging shoes can lead to problems, such as joint pain, sore knees and foot pain.

Your shoes might not look worn out, but often the damage done to them is on the inside

YOUR BIOMECHANICS

Whether you are running on roads, a treadmill or elsewhere, a key factor to what shoe you will need will be your personal biomechanics.

When your foot hits the ground, it is likely to be on the outside of the heel. The foot then rolls inwards to be flat on the ground. This rolling motion - called 'pronation' - absorbs shock and gives you balance as you run. However, it is very common for a runner to have their foot roll too far as they run. This is called 'over-pronation'. Working out whether you over-pronate is quite straight forward and there is no need to worry if you find you do. It is a very common trait and there are plenty of shoes designed to help manage your footstrike, keep you comfortable and help you avoid injury.

The Ultimate Guide to Marathon Running

THE OLD SHOE TEST

Take a look at a pair of your old shoes to see what kind of shoes you need:

Stand them on a level surface and look at them from behind the heel.

If you over-pronate, your shoes will show a slight inward lean. You need 'support' or 'motion control' shoes if your feet roll too far. Many people make the mistake of looking at wear on the outsole, at the outside of the heel, and thinking they don't over-pronate. This wear is caused on landing and does not relate to pronation.

Under-pronation is when a runner's foot does not roll far enough. If you under-pronate, your shoes will show a slight outwards lean. Choose a pair of cushioning shoes.

Correct pronation means there won't be any lean. Your feet are said to be neutral. You should choose 'neutral' shoes.

If you have run in 'support' shoes in the past, not had injury problems and your shoes show no signs of inwards lean, it probably means you do need 'support' shoes, but the shoes have successfully prevented the over-pronation in the past.

The shoe categories

We can divide running shoes into the following categories:

SUPPORT
These have the same kind of cushioning technologies as neutral shoes, but they also have features to give extra support and guidance to slow and reduce over-pronation.

Brooks Adrenalin GTS 12

adizero tempo

RACERS
Made for racing or very fast training (e.g. track work). These shoes are very light, but offer limited protection. Some offer support for over-pronators.

MOTION CONTROL
People who over-pronate more severely and heavier runners who over-pronate can choose these shoes, which provide extra support and guidance.

NEUTRAL
These are for runners who are neutral or under-pronate. Some shoes may also be suitable for mild over-pronators. Under-pronators should look for a pair of well-cushioned neutral shoes.

Asics Gel Kinsei 3

LIGHTWEIGHTS
For use in fast training or racing, these offer less protection than regular training shoes. They are also either neutral or supportive.

Mizuno Wave Alchemy 11

New Balance Revlite

The Ultimate Guide to Marathon Running

ESSENTIAL KIT

Trail/off-road shoes

ROAD RUNNING is one of the most popular sports in the UK. Hundreds of thousands of people line up for road races each year and many, many more will run on the roads to exercise.

But most of us who run regularly also enjoy taking opportunities to run off-road for a change of surface and scenery. If we are only heading on to lighter trails, a standard pair of road-running shoes will usually be fine. In fact, many of them are designed in the knowledge that runners don't stick rigidly to the pavement.

But if you head for something a little more demanding, or start putting in more of your miles on the trails, it is often worth buying a pair of trail-specific shoes. These have grip tailored to off-road conditions; they also have a midsole and upper designed to keep your foot stable and secure when the ground is uneven.

Runners can also benefit from turning to off-road races. Top British distance runners, from 800m specialists such as Seb Coe to marathon legends such as Paula Radcliffe, have all wintered on the cross country.

But the diversity of off-road events is now greater than ever. The distances in off-road events are usually non-standard, meaning you can just focus on racing and not get too hung up on the stopwatch. They are often more undulating, which gives a great opportunity for building endurance, and running downhill is an effective way of building fast, relaxed technique and improving leg speed. Other events, such as the GRIM Challenge, really take getting muddy to new lengths. Fell races take the hills to the extreme and ultra events can give a different challenge to those wanting to breakaway from the more mainstream running events.

But, whatever experience you choose, the right footwear is essential. Fortunately, there is a wide variety of shoes for fell running and off-road races. These are lighter than standard trail shoes (although there is actually a full spectrum of shoes available) and often have a lower-profile midsole to give stability without weight.

Running and training off-road should be a regular part of your marathon programme.

But whatever you do, make sure you have chosen the best shoes for your needs to ensure you get maximum enjoyment from your run.

HAPPY LANDING

If you want to know what type of runner you are, video analysis is a great way of identifying your gait. If this isn't available, just get someone to watch how your foot lands to work out whether you are:

A rearfoot striker
This is the most common way to land, on your heel first before rolling up through the rest of your foot. Rearfoot strikers tend to have a slower foot turnover (the time between the foot hitting and leaving the ground), which could mean slower per-mile times.

TOP TIP: look for more cushioning at the rear of the shoe to absorb the shock for your heel.

A midfoot striker
This person lands near the midsection of the foot so that the back of the heel never actually strikes the ground. The shock is equally absorbed and most midfoot strikers are less likely to get injured.

TOP TIP: look for cushioning and support at the heel and the toe of the shoe.

A forefoot striker
This tends to be the category most elite runners fall into. Forefoot strikers have a fast turnover, which means they run faster - their heels never touch the ground. New shoes, such as the Newton, have been introduced to encourage rearfoot and midfoot strikers to run on their toes.

TOP TIP: look for extra cushioning in the forefoot or try Newton shoes.

The Ultimate Guide to Marathon Running

Quite literally the making of champions

JJ Jegede — Long Jump
"Since using **wellman** I have become indoor UK **No. 1**"

Rhys Williams — 400m Hurdles
"The training demands in my sport are very high and without the Wellman® nutritional supplements I COULD NOT ACHIEVE MY FULL POTENTIAL."

Sophie Hitchon — Hammer
before taking **wellwoman** UK No.2 NOW **No.1***

Alison Waters — Squash
"Wellwoman is working. Alison is stronger than I have ever seen her."
Gordon Kerr, Manager
WORLD **No.3**††

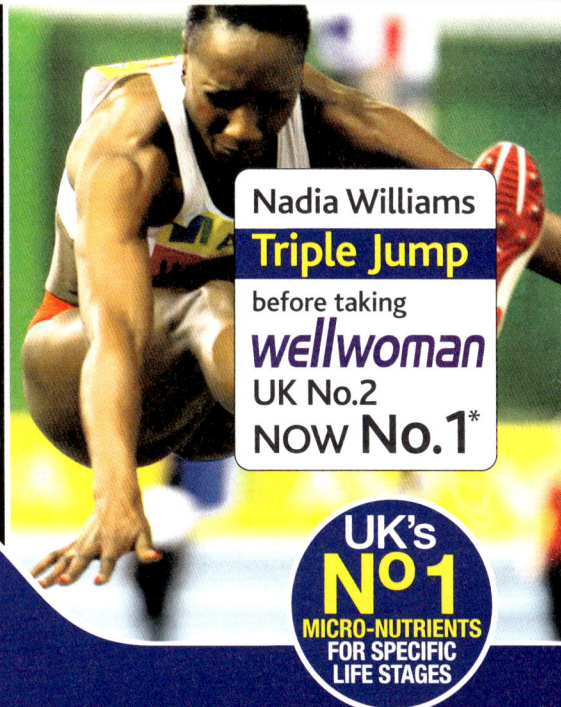

Nadia Williams — Triple Jump
before taking **wellwoman** UK No.2 NOW **No.1***

With under one year to go, Vitabiotics is set to astound the world of sport

UK's No 1 MICRO-NUTRIENTS FOR SPECIFIC LIFE STAGES

NEW Wellman® Optimuscle®
The science behind lean muscle power
New at **GNC**

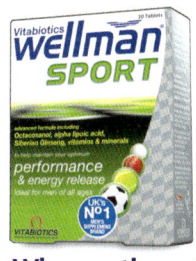

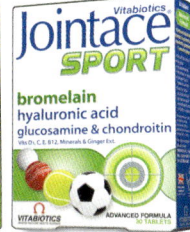

Also from at health stores, pharmacies & www.vitabiotics.com. *June 2011. †May 2011. ††February 2011
Vitamin supplements may benefit those with nutritionally inadequate diets.

Why are these Great Britain athletes all moving up the rankings so quickly?
Determination and raw talent – combined with Vitabiotics' sports supplements. Developed by experts, new *Optimuscle®* offers three advanced formulations to support your training requirements.

Britain's leading supplements for specific life stages

VITABIOTICS
WHERE NATURE MEETS SCIENCE

● ESSENTIAL KIT

The Ultimate Guide to Marathon Running

DRESSING FOR WARM-WEATHER RUNNING

WHEN RUNNING in warm weather, the right clothing can help you stay cool and comfortable. You will need less clothing – perhaps a vest or crop top instead of a T-shirt. Remember to wear sunscreen of at least factor 15 on all exposed areas of your skin.

THE TYPE of fabric your clothes are made from can also affect your comfort. Cotton has the advantage of being cheap and is quick to soak up sweat as you run, but it retains this moisture, which makes it heavy and wet during exercise. Also, cotton T-shirts often have rough, uneven stitching, which can cause chafing and, in extreme cases, bleeding.

IF YOU are going to wear cotton, it's probably best to opt for lightweight cotton because a dense weave, heavyweight material will feel heavy more quickly. Lightweight cotton will also chafe less than heavier fabric.

WICKING FABRICS are an alternative to cotton. These are man-made fabrics designed to draw sweat away from the skin to the outer surface so that it can easily evaporate. This means that clothing stays light and feels dry. Companies that specialise in running clothing will also include other design features for the comfort of the runner, such as mesh inserts for ventilation. 'Technical' clothes are likely to be more expensive, so it's up to you to decide whether the extra comfort is worth the expense.

DRESSING FOR COLD-WEATHER RUNNING

LAYERING IS the key to staying comfortable in cold conditions because air is trapped between the layers of clothing and acts as insulation. You can take layers off as you warm up.

MOST RUNNERS opt for three layers if cold-weather running. Start with a light base layer, preferably of a wicking material to draw sweat away from your body. It should be a snug fit but not too tight or restrictive. This could be a crop top or vest, or a long-sleeved top, depending on the conditions.

THE NEXT layer could be a lightweight long-sleeved top. In milder weather, this can be your outer garment. It's a good idea if this is a wicking fabric too and it should fit loosely over the base layer so that trapped air between the two layers will create insulation. In extreme cold, or if you don't wear a third layer, the second layer could be a lightweight fleece.

YOUR THIRD layer depends on the weather. If it's very cold, windy, raining or snowing, opt for a breathable, windproof, water-resistant jacket. This should fit loosely.

YOU MAY want to wear lightweight training trousers or leggings rather than shorts. The type you buy will depend on the weather conditions. For example, you can buy water-resistant trousers for wet weather and fleece-lined ones for particularly cold weather. Again, depending on the weather conditions, you can put a pair of water-resistant trousers on top.

MODERN RUNNING clothing has come on leaps and bounds since the days of cotton t-shirts. intelligent fabrics can help keep you cool in the summer

The Ultimate Guide to Marathon Running

● ESSENTIAL KIT

Summer

1. ASICS Light Short Sleeve Top £30
➤ www.asics.co.uk

2. Adidas Supernova Tank £28
➤ www.adidas.co.uk

3. Ronhill Aspiration Shortsleeve Tee
➤ www.ronhill.com

4. Ronhill Women's Trail Twin Short £35.50
➤ www.ronhill.com

5. Helly Hansen Pace Shorts £30
➤ www.hellyhansen.co.uk

DRESS TO IMPRESS!

Winter

1. Mizuno Performance Jacket £60
➤ www.mizuno.co.uk

2. Brooks Equilibrium LS Top £24
➤ www.brooksrunning.co.uk

3. Nike Swift Power Men's Running Tights £50
➤ www.nikestore.com

4. Nike Element Shield Men's Running Jacket £90
➤ www.nikestore.com

5. Ronhill Vizion Windlite Jacket £50
➤ www.ronhill.com

The Ultimate Guide to Marathon Running

pure project
BROOKS
PureFlow
The beginning of something beautiful.
run happy
BROOKS
www.brookspureproject.co.uk

● ESSENTIAL KIT

Hats and gloves

IF YOU'RE training for a spring marathon, the likelihood is that you'll be knocking out the bulk of your miles in the inclement weather that has come to typify a UK winter.

Given that the winter of 2008/09 was one of the coldest on record (January temperatures barely rose above freezing), you'll be wanting to reach for anything that helps protect you from the elements: after all, we lose most of our body heat through our heads, right? In fact - although our head and chest are particularly sensitive to temperature changes - no one body part loses more heat than any other. Only about 10% of the body's heat escapes from an uncovered head, much lower than the 40-80% we have been told (and have told others) since the army released the claim in a survival manual during the 1970s. Still, wearing a hat can make a long run in the freezing cold more bearable. Likewise, you might want to wear a hat with a visor in the summer to protect your eyes from the sun's rays and to reflect the heat (providing it's a light colour), although I tend to find that this makes me hotter and impedes my body's capacity to sweat. It's also plain uncomfortable.

Gloves are very much a personal preference. But, for runners with poor circulation (and I'm one of them), gloves are an essential part of a winter wardrobe. Many people find that their hands heat up too much when wearing gloves and they're forced to throw them at an unsuspecting friend or tuck them into their shorts (not always the most comfortable option). During the marathon race, you'll have a fairly high core-body temperature and you may be wearing just a singlet and shorts. But as the race wears on and you lose energy stores, especially if conditions worsen (i.e. increased wind), your body can't maintain that higher temperature and you can become hypothermic. Some runners will keep on gloves and a hat throughout the race to guard against that.

Contrary to popular belief, you don't lose all your heat through your head, but runners with poor circulation will welcome the warming effects of hats and gloves in winter

You'll want your socks to be lightweight and as cushioned as possible, particularly on the heel and forefoot, which will see the most action

Socks

They might seem like the least exciting accessory on the market, but wearing the right pair of socks can make all the difference to your marathon performance.

If you want to avoid blisters - or at least minimise the possibility of getting them - choosing your socks carefully should be pretty high on your list of priorities.

Sock technology has come on in leaps and bounds: today's high-tech running socks have different material thicknesses at key points and different fabrics where, for example, you might need extra elasticity.

You'll want your socks to be lightweight - there's no point carrying any extra weight for 26.2 miles - and you'll want them as cushioned as possible, particularly on the heel and forefoot, which will see the most action during the run.

Look for high-tech fabrics such as CoolMax, a moisture management fabric that helps move moisture away from the skin and keeps your feet cool, dry and comfortable. Some socks have a double layer that helps prevent friction: the inner sock wicks moisture to the outer cotton sock, keeping the skin dry and reducing the onset of blisters.

While most runners prefer a sock that fits low around their ankle, increasingly you'll see runners wearing knee-high compression socks (see 'Compression Clothing'). These are designed to reduce calf and Achilles problems, and reduce muscle vibration - which can be excessive through the course of the marathon distance.

The Ultimate Guide to Marathon Running

Sunglasses

PAULA RADCLIFFE wears them; so does former Olympic and World 400m champion Jeremy Wariner. The market for performance eyewear has exploded in the past 10 years, particularly in cycling and triathlon, in which athletes of all abilities have recognised the benefits that can be derived from wearing sunglasses.

Yet, when it comes to running, performance eyewear tends to be limited to the upper echelons of ability. This may come down to a number of reasons. People might be put off by cost - yet there are some excellent sunglasses available at the £40-£50 price point. Then there's the look: many people perceive sports sunglasses to be wholly cosmetic. But they're missing the point.

While manufacturers try to make their products as aesthetically pleasing as possible, this is not their principle aim. More time, money and effort goes into lens technology and the performance and efficacy of eyewear than how it looks, which is great news for those who wear them, because they're getting real value for money.

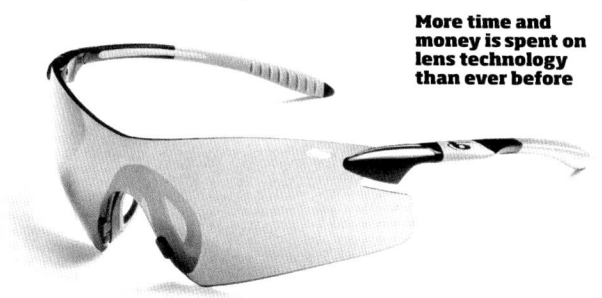

More time and money is spent on lens technology than ever before

Protection

THE MOST basic levels of protection are from UVA, UVB and UVC rays. This protection is essential because the eye - like our skin - can be seriously damaged by these rays. As the cornea is one of the most sensitive areas on the body, it is as likely as the skin to be damaged. Admittedly, this level of protection is something most off-the-rack sunglasses will also protect against, though many do not counteract the effects of 'blue light' - a newly identified condition, detrimental to the eye.

Additionally, performance eyewear can offer protection from the elements, flying debris and vision distortion thanks to their lenses, which should wrap around the face, be made from high-grade, impact-resistant materials and utilise appropriate lens technology for varying conditions. This level of protection may seem basic, but the average set of sunglasses is not designed for variable conditions.

What are the key benefits of sunglasses?

1 Running can put tremendous strain on the eyes. A pair of running sunglasses is a must for anyone who takes their running seriously. The human eye is not designed to allow a lot of air to pass at speed for lengthy periods of time. Some running sunglasses have filters to counter excess wind; others will just deflect away wind from the eye.

2 When running, you can be subjected to glare from the road and also be exposed to long periods of sunlight. This can cause you to squint, resulting in tension in the face that can affect the rest of your body. Wearing sunglasses can help block the glare.

3 Getting foreign objects in your eye can be painful and, potentially, threaten your race performance. Wearing sunglasses can help alleviate the problem of dust coming up off the road in a race or training.

4 The sun's rays can be extremely harmful. Wearing a pair of sunglasses can protect the eyes from UVA and UVB light.

5 Sports glasses come with interchangeable lenses, which means you can wear them when the sun isn't shining to help keep rain and the other, more hostile, elements of the British weather out of your eyes. Special, hydroponic lenses help to keep out the water.

Top tips for choosing performance eyewear

Here are few simple things you should look for when selecting sunglasses for running:

LENS TECHNOLOGY - Do the glasses provide a clear view, without distortion, across the full lens, not just in one 'optical sweetspot'? Is the tint/colour appropriate for the conditions/use and do they enhance your vision?

ANTI-FOG COATING - Anti-fog coating on lenses is usually standard with most manufacturers.

ARMS - Are the arms of the glasses adjustable to create a 'best fit' around your temples? Are they also detachable in case of accident or impact?

COMFORT AND FIT - Do the glasses sit snugly, yet comfortably, on your face? Do the contact points grip without feeling too tight? Make sure the glasses are not too big or loose because this will create movement on the run.

LIGHTWEIGHT - Are the glasses light in comparison to other similar models at that price point? The lighter the glasses, the more comfortable they are likely to be over long runs.

NOSE-PIECE - Does it fit the shape of your nose and is it adjustable and comfortable? Runners often have a problem with glasses slipping down because of poor-quality nose-pieces.

PRESCRIPTION COMPATIBLE - Can the frame take a prescription if you need or develop the need for one?

UV AND BLUE LIGHT PROTECTION - Do they provide 100% UV A,B and C protection? Additionally, do they filter out blue light, which, experts inform us, can cause serious damage to eyes?

VENTILATION - When on, the glasses should not fit so closely that there is no room for air-flow to ventilate them.

VERSATILE LENS FITTED/ INTERCHANGEABLE LENS OPTIONS - Do the glasses come with a lens that is versatile in most conditions - or do they give the option to swap lenses in the frame? In the latter case, do the glasses come with a second lens? Additional lenses can be costly.

● ESSENTIAL **KIT**

Sports bra

LIKE WOMEN'S shoes and clothing, the science behind sports bras has raced ahead in recent years. Specialist bra manufacturers have worked hard to increase the levels of support offered by their garments to prevent women from damaging their breasts during running.

Yet it's something of a surprise to find many women still eschew a decent sports bra in favour of an everyday variety – or, sometimes, nothing at all! An alarming three quarters (76 per cent) of active British women admit they do not regularly wear a sports bra when exercising, according to a recent study. More than a third (34 per cent) of those questioned do not wear a sports bra because they are worried about looking good while exercising.

The research by Shock Absorber found one sixth claim they don't like how a sports bra looks, 12 per cent don't think sports bras give their breasts the right shape and style-conscious seven per cent won't wear one if it doesn't match their outfit.

The study also revealed many women were unsure when they needed to wear a sports bra. More than four fifths (85 per cent) wouldn't wear a sports bra for yoga or Pilates, two fifths wouldn't wear one for a dance exercise class and nearly one in five (18 per cent) wouldn't even wear a sports bra when running.

And yet, during exercise, research has shown that breasts move in a three-dimensional movement, going up and down, in and out, and side to side. With the average 36C breast weighing between 250-300grams, this movement puts great strain on the breast's fragile support structure, which comprises only the outer skin and connective tissue known as Cooper's ligament. Breast movement can cause the Cooper's ligaments to stretch and this can lead to irreversible damage to the breasts.

During the transition phase from walking to running, 3D bounce increases rapidly, then levels off. The implication of this is that you need a sports bra just as much at lower running speeds as at high speeds.

OUR CHOICE

**Shockabsorber Flexi-wire sports bra
£32 www.shockabsorber.co.uk**

To appeal to image-conscious fitness fans, Shock Absorber has created the revolutionary Flexi-wire sports bra, which feels as comfortable and looks as good as a regular bra yet has all the support and features of a sports bra. The flexi-wire, which is a non-rigid titanium memory underwire, will not bend out of shape with wash and wear. The slim, padded straps which can be worn as a straight or racer back and neat cut design make the bra easy to wear for all types of exercise and under all sports tops.

BEST OF THE REST

Adidas Nandinia Racer Bra £28
www.adidas.com
Excellent levels of support, well designed and very comfortable. The highlight is the breathable and lightweight fabric.

Triumph Extreme Tri Action £28
www.triumphlingeriestore.com
Comfortable, a good fit and made from soft breathable fabric with no annoying itchy seams or labels.

Moving Comfort Fiona Bra £29.99
www.movingcomfort.com
This moisture-wicking, quick-drying and breathable bra has an inner structure that provides maximum support and comfort.

The Ultimate Guide to Marathon Running

HOW TO CHOOSE AND FIT YOUR BRA PROPERLY
By Shock Absorber expert Kirsty Kothokota

■ Invest in a quality product made of a moisture wicking performance sports fabric that is quick dry and breathable.

■ If you have never worn a sports bra before, start off with the same bra size you would normally wear

■ Make sure that the back band is at the same level all the way round. If it rides up, then it's too big. It should feel firm. Always fit your bra to the loosest hook and eye. That way you can adjust it to make it tighter as it stretches with wash and wear.

■ Is your bust fully contained within the cups with no overspill and no bagginess?

■ Do the bounce test! Jump up and down: this is the best way to test out the support. Still too much bounce? Try on another size to get the right fit.

● ESSENTIAL KIT

COMPRESSION CLOTHING

Runners tend to wear clothing that is comfortable, breathable, wicks sweat away from the skin to prevent chaffing, gives good mobility and keeps them at a good temperature.

These criteria are vitally important, but new factors have added to the diversity of products on offer.

'Compression clothing' is often used as a generic name for a range of products and it's important to understand the differences between what's on offer. Some of it is 'true' compression clothing, whereas other items are functional pieces of kit that are tight-fitting.

Applying a suitable amount of pressure to a muscle increases circulation to it - known as improved micro-circulation

Technologies have been developed to improve posture and give a resistance that strengthens key, but hard to train, muscles

The less soreness you have after training, the sooner you will be prepared for that next session

The right materials, the right cut and exactly the correct size are important when choosing compression clothing

1 PROPRIOCEPTION
Proprioception is about being aware of your body, its posture and its movement. It is possible to wear clothing that increases this awareness and, therefore, improves your posture and technique as you train and compete.

2 CIRCULATION
This is a more difficult goal to achieve. Applying a suitable amount of pressure to a muscle increases circulation to it – improved micro-circulation. Think of the principle behind the socks you can buy to prevent deep vein thrombosis on long aeroplane flights. Doing the same during exercise can boost your performance because the extra blood helps fuel your muscles and remove waste products.

You can also wear the clothing between sessions to gain the same benefits – weary legs are flushed out and recovery enhanced. Sleeping in the clothing or wearing it under your regular clothing allows you to go into the next session fresher.

Of course there's always a catch when something sounds this good... improved micro-circulation is a more difficult benefit to achieve than increased proprioception. If you use inadequate pressure, circulation is not stimulated. Too much pressure will have the opposite effect – circulation will be hindered!

The right materials, the right cut and wearing exactly the correct size become very important. Hence, you will see far more complex sizing charts for clothing that can really deliver on this front.

3 MUSCLE VIBRATION
If you watch a very-slow-motion film of a runner, you will see their muscles vibrate and oscillate as they run. It is believed that reducing this oscillation and vibration may reduce the strain on the muscles during exercise and so reduce delayed onset muscle soreness (DOMS) - in other words, feeling as stiff as a board a while after exercise. The less soreness you have after training, the sooner you will be ready to tackle that next session.

4 TECHNICAL ADVANCES
As material technology and biomechanical understanding increase, the boffins come up with more and more ways of applying the know-how. At ASICS, Inner Muscle technologies have been developed to improve posture and give resistance that strengthens key, but hard to train, muscles. Adidas, meanwhile, has spotted that by adding a Powerweb (a polymer overlay that works like hi-tech rubber bands) to its clothing, athletes can improve their posture and the power they can generate. A lot of the power generated when you run is from 'elastic energy' - for example, from stretching and releasing your Achilles tendon. The Adidas Powerwebbing seeks to add to that energy.

The Ultimate Guide to Marathon Running

SHOCK ABSORBER
FIT TO RUN!

Shock Absorber is committed to making your marathon performance the best it can be.

Whether it's your first marathon or you're a seasoned running pro, a Shock Absorber sports bra is an essential piece of running kit.

■ THE EXPERTS

Shock Absorber is the UK's leading sports bra brand and provides the expert support to female runners. Always at the forefront of sports bra innovation, Shock Absorber understands the requirements a female runner needs when taking part in marathons.

■ DESIGNED FOR RUNNING

Our extensive research on running show that breasts move in a continuous figure of eight pattern, putting repetitive strain on the Coopers ligament in the breast. With 18 months of research and technical design Shock Absorber developed the ground breaking RUN bra.

■ REVOLUTIONARY DESIGN

Shock Absorber's high-performance RUN bra boasts the new Infinity-8 support to prevent a figure of eight movement your breasts make during running and has proven to reduce breast bounce by up to 78%*. The revolutionary RUN bra includes a soft, seam-free inner lining to reduce the rubbing and chafing, wide and padded non-slip straps so your bra always stays in place and moisture-wicking, advanced sports performance fabrics.

SHOCK ABSORBER RUN BRA £37

The Shock Absorber RUN bra costs £37 and is available in sizes 30 – 36 A and 30 – 38 B to F. Available in black or white and limited edition in red/white/blue, and can be purchased from major department stores, sports shops and online retailers. **To find your nearest stockist visit www.shockabsorber.co.uk**

Join the Shock Absorber UK community on Facebook.

*University of Portsmouth 2009 (Scurr et al) - testing carried out against 'no bra' conditions.

ESSENTIAL KIT

Watches and heart-rate monitors

EXPERIENCE SHOWS that most people, when they first start running, tend to follow a distance-based method of training and shy away from time-based or heart rate-based methods. This is because the latter are perceived as complex and costly, and there's a lack of training programmes to follow.

A common occurrence is for beginners to buy a heart-rate monitor (HRM) because they know it's of use, but then end up using it just as a watch - and to amaze their friends with how high their heart rate goes (or low, if you're being really clever!).

But running to a heart-rate or using a watch to time repetitions or training runs is not something to be frightened of. If you want to know what to look for, here's some handy advice.

WHAT TO LOOK FOR IN A SPORTS WATCH

Here are a few key features to look for when choosing a sports watch to help you get the most out of your training:

DATA MEMORY
This function, once the preserve of top-end gadgets, is fast becoming the norm for all sports watches. It allows you to record all of the lap (and other) data from your training session, to revisit it later when you're analysing what you have done.

INTERVAL SETTING
This is a key function for getting the most out of your watch. It counts down a set time-span or, in the case of top-end watches, a set pattern of time spans and then beeps to let you know that the interval has been completed. On some watches, this is referred to as a countdown timer.

CHRONOGRAPH
This is the basic stopwatch function and a prerequisite of any sports watch.

LAP TIMING
This is a function usually found within the chronograph setting of the watch. It'll allow you to split the time readings as you go through a session and should allow you to see the overall time and the current lap you are on. This can be very useful when interval training by distance or when racing, when you may want to record and judge your pace over set distances or efforts. Top-end watches often have memory or capacity for 200 lap times, although 50 should suit the needs of most runners.

ERGONOMICS
Look for a watch that's comfortable on your wrist, ideally with a vented strap to allow perspiration to disperse. The watch face/screen should be easily readable when running and the buttons easy to work when on the move.

WHEN SELECTING A HEART-RATE MONITOR, LOOK OUT FOR:

A GOOD SPORTS WATCH -
This goes without saying; a good HRM should have all the functions of a sports watch. There's no reason to wear two watches on your wrist.

COMFORTABLE AND UNIQUELY CODED HEART-RATE BELT -
Heart-rate monitors read your heart via a belt that sits around your chest, so it's important to ensure that the belt is going to be comfortable and not rub or chafe. It should also have a unique electronic code that's matched to the wrist piece, so, when you're out training, the monitor doesn't pick up someone else's readings.

CURRENT HEART-RATE FUNCTION -
This function tells you what your heart rate is at the time and is important when trying to work in a specific zone.

AVERAGE HEART-RATE FUNCTION -
This calculates the average heart rate over a session and is useful when trying to gauge actual fitness.

MAXIMUM HEART-RATE FUNCTION -
This function simply records the highest heart rate over the course of a session.

PROGRAMMABLE HEART-RATE TRAINING ZONE ALARM -
This is a hugely useful function that allows you to programme the desired range for a workout and, if you drop below or go above that, it beeps to let you know you're out of the zone.

* Other desirable functions can include the ability to download the recorded data onto a computer. This is useful because it allows you keep a record of your sessions and measure your improvement.

Soleus Running GPS 1.0 £99

Having listened to runners around the world, Soleus has only included functions in the GPS 1.0 that give users instant feedback. The unit is easy-to-use, picks up the satellite signal quickly and then provides up-to-the-minute feedback on speed, distance, pace and calories burned. It also includes a handy auto-lap feature that allows the user to programme pre-determined markers (for example, mile splits) that automatically record and store the time, pace, distance at each marker - useful if you want to check your stats immediately after your run. The GPS watch also features a 50-lap memory chronograph, a world time facility and a rechargeable battery with an 8-hour charge. It is also water-resistant to 30 metres.

➤ **www.fitbrands.co.uk**

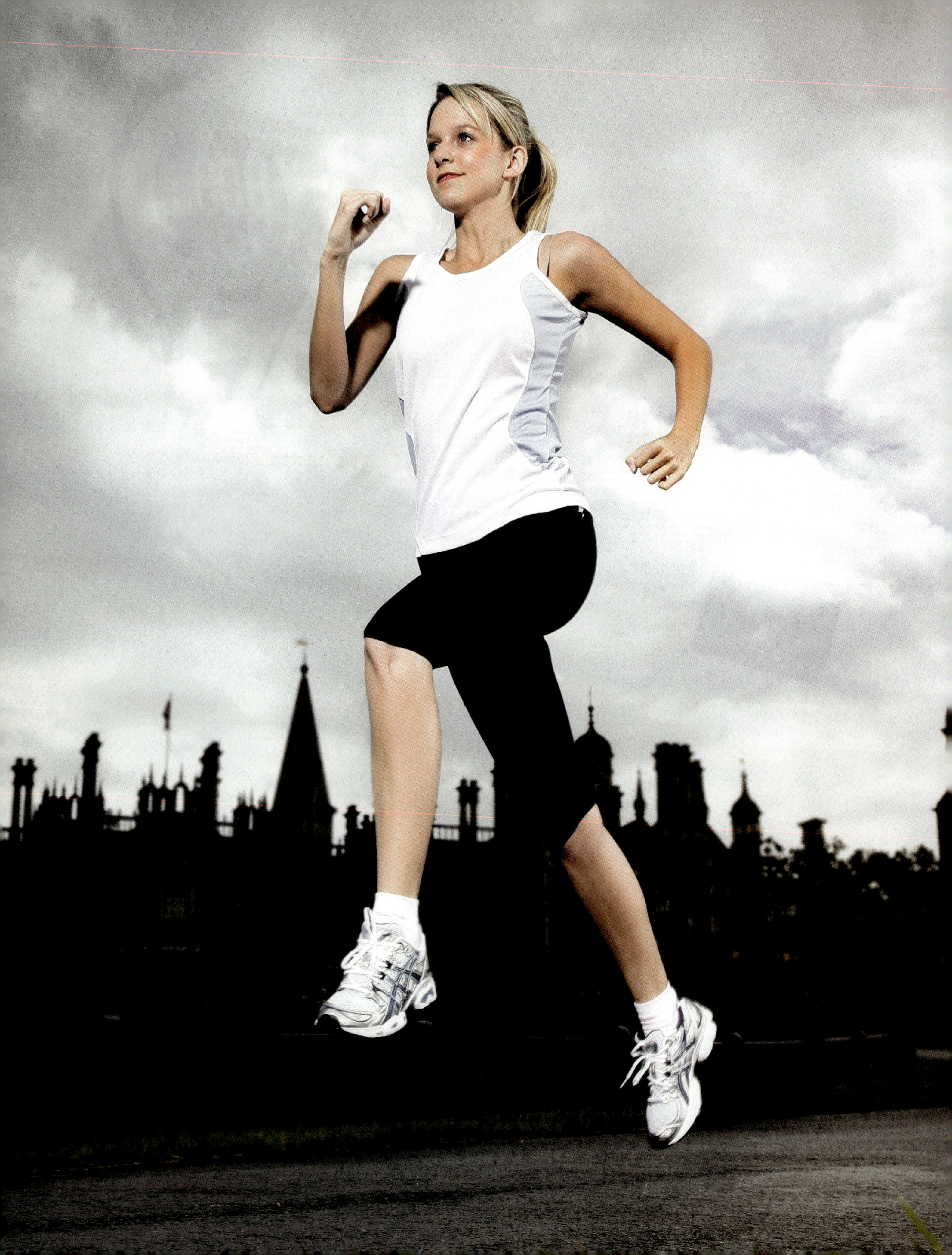

Part three
STARTING TRAINING

If you thought you could get round 26.2 miles with no training, think again. The fact that you're reading this chapter is more than enough evidence that you've decided to opt for the sensible route and train your body for the rigours of a marathon. We might have said it on more than one occasion already, but marathon running isn't easy. The training formula may not be as simplistic as saying the more you do, the easier it will be, but it's not far off. It should come as no surprise that the likes of Paula Radcliffe run more than 120 miles a week. Before you start thinking that's what you need to do, remember your goals: if you want to run under three hours, you're going to need to put in a fair bit of training. But it's all relative and also dependent on your running and sporting history. If you're fit, healthy and prepared to work hard, you will achieve your goal – and perhaps surprise yourself.

> **RUNNING IS A BIG QUESTION MARK THAT'S THERE EACH AND EVERY DAY. IT ASKS YOU, 'ARE YOU GOING TO BE A WIMP OR ARE YOU GOING TO BE STRONG?'** — ELITE MARATHONER

The Ultimate Guide to Marathon Running

● STARTING TRAINING

Surfaces ● Treadmill running ● Training terms ● Recovery

WHAT SHOULD YOU EXPECT?

If you have never trained for a marathon, there's one thing you can be sure of: it's not easy. Quite apart from the physical torments of actually putting in the mileage for your particular goal, there's the constant mental fatigue from worrying that you're doing too much or too little, being on the verge of injury or illness, or - for all those first-timers - wondering whether you'll actually be able to complete the distance.

We might not be able to take away all of these, but we can certainly provide you with the right coping mechanisms to be able to stay the course - the first being the training.

Training theories have come a long way over the past 60 years: you only have to look at how much the marathon world bests have improved for evidence of that (the men's world best was 2hrs 25mins 39secs in 1947: it's now an astonishing 2hrs 3mins 59secs, run by Haile Gebrselassie).

While they are an individual thing, there tends to be common elements to all training programmes, no matter how fast or slow you expect to cover the marathon distance. Most marathon training programmes will last for at least three months and it is recommended that you do some type of running before you even start your marathon training. In fact, before you begin marathon training, you should be able to run for at least 30 minutes without stopping. Distance is not important right now - you just need to get your body used to running. Combinations of runs/walks are great to use during pre-training because they ease your body into the exercise and minimise the chance of experiencing a running-related injury.

The most important thing to remember is that your training will be progressive - don't expect to start running high mileage in week one. Structured training is exactly that: it is designed to get your body used to the rigours of running a marathon by progressively stepping up your training load. Typically, your training will fall into three phases: a build phase, a consolidation and a taper.

During the build phase, you're laying down the foundations for the harder training you will be doing; in the consolidation phase, you'll be completing the longer runs, tempo sessions and speed work that will determine your final race performance; and, in the taper phase, you'll be recovering - and letting your body 'process' all of that hard training!

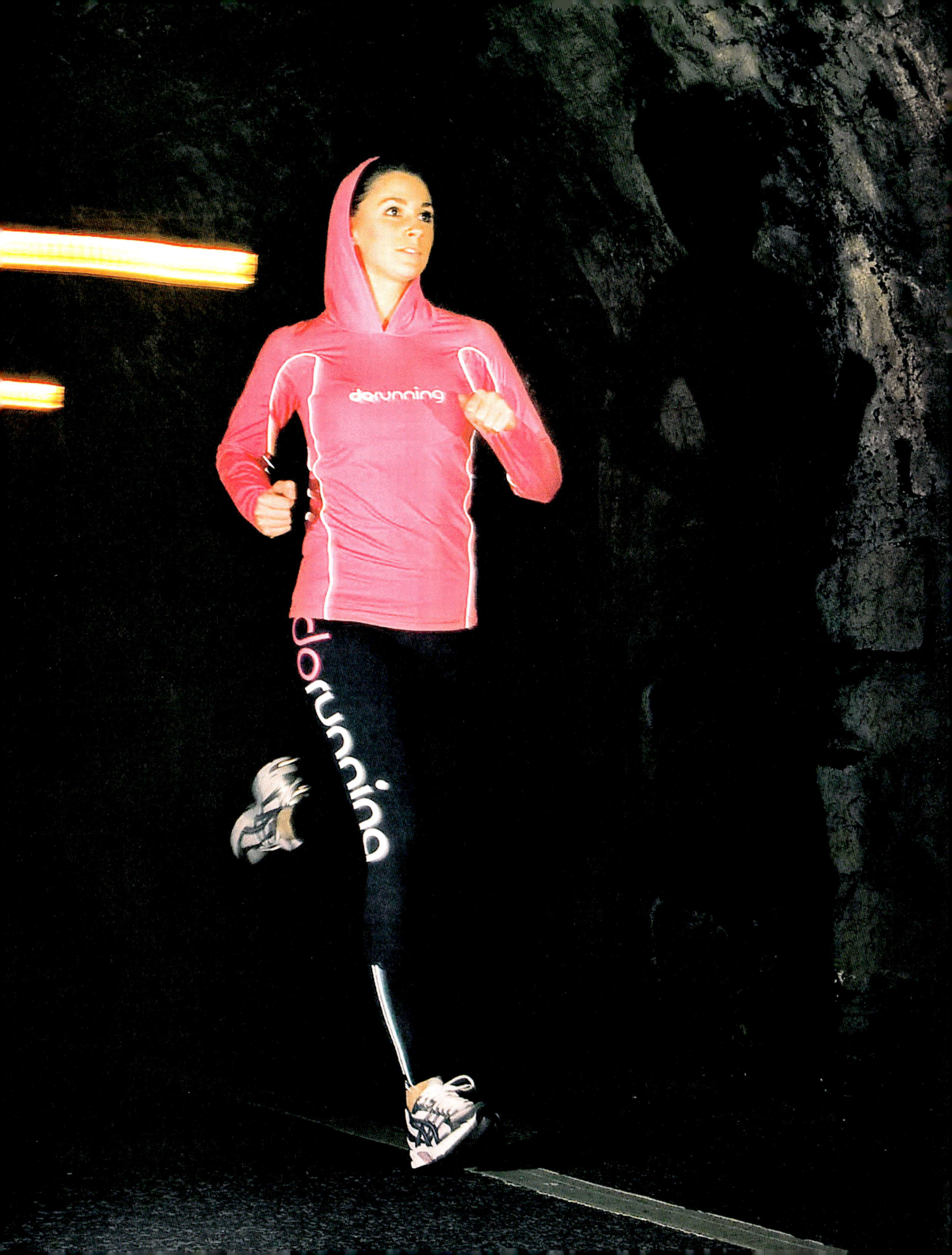
dorunning
dorunning

● STARTING TRAINING

What's underfoot?

IF YOU'RE going to take up the challenge of completing the marathon distance, you're going to be doing some long runs in training. The length, speed and frequency of these is, obviously, dependent on your ultimate goal.

Nevertheless, if you follow a training plan (like one of those featured in this book), you'll find that, at various stages of your programme, you'll be running at least 15 miles – probably up to 20 and, possibly, beyond.

Now, you could take your favourite five-mile route and simply run around it three or four times. But that could become a trifle tiresome. The beauty of running is that you can do it on just about any surface, anywhere – and each surface has its own particular merits.

If you're planning on running a big city marathon, you'll be running 26.2 miles on the road. While this is great for race day (faster times, less likely to trip over roots), it is about the least forgiving of all running surfaces.

Given the potential for injury with running – and with marathon training in particular – it is far better to mix up your surfaces and protect your joints, muscles and limbs in the process. It will also help alleviate the boredom of logging mile after mile on the road.

TOP FIVE REASONS FOR MIXING UP RUNNING SURFACES

INJURY PREVENTION: running all your marathon training on hard surfaces increases the amount of force put through your joints and muscles. Running off-road, on grass or trails, alleviates the stress on the body and means you're less likely to incur over-use injuries.

RELIEVE BOREDOM: there's no denying that training can become repetitive. Running on different surfaces can help inject some variety into your training.

SEE THE WORLD: discovering new routes is part of the enjoyment of running. By venturing onto woodland paths, coastal trails or seaside lanes, you'll find new routes that will make your runs a voyage of discovery.

GETTING AWAY FROM IT ALL: many people like to use their running as 'me' time, to put the troubles of the world behind them and detox from the rigours of life. Running away from busy roads and populated paths helps relieve stress (although, for men and women, there's a point to be raised here about safety. Always let someone know where you are going and carry some ID).

INJURY PREVENTION: yes, we've said it already, but don't underestimate the potential for injury if all your runs are done on hard surfaces. Variety is the spice of life!

The Ultimate Guide to Marathon Running

GRASS

My personal favourite — and that of many runners — grassland, such as parks, golf courses and football pitches, provides an excellent surface for running.

Pros: While grass is soft and easy on the legs in terms of impact, it actually makes your muscles work hard. This builds strength and means you'll notice a difference when you return to the road. It's great for reps and more forgiving than the track.

Cons: Some grassland is uneven and can be dangerous for runners with unstable ankles. It can also be slippery when wet, runners with allergies may suffer more symptoms when running on it and its softness can tire legs surprisingly quickly.

Conclusion: If you can find a flat, even stretch of it, grass is the best training surface for most runners, especially as you get older.

WOODLAND TRAILS

If you can find a section big enough (the Forestry Commission has turned a number of forests, such as Bedgebury Pinetum, into walking, running and cycling areas), the softer ground and constantly changing environs are ideal for running. They can be firm, but may also be shared with horses and cyclists.

Pros: Usually easy on the legs and located in scenic areas that make you keen to return.

Cons: Unless you're lucky enough to find wood chips or well-drained peat, woodland trails can be muddy and slippery, especially those with larger volumes of traffic, including horses.

Conclusion: A woodchip trail can make a fantastic run – softer ground, spectacular scenery and marked paths – but it's not easy to find an area big enough, especially for a long run.

The Ultimate Guide to Marathon Running

HAVE YOU GOT WHAT IT TAKES TO CHANGE?

Whether you are working towards your ideal physique in terms of appearance or whether you need your physique to deliver increased performance, you have a challenge on your hands.

Without maximizing each important component, you are likely to compromise or fail in your goals. When it comes to supplements, you might well need to change your views.

If you don't change your views, you may already have failed in your goals.

- We've changed the industry standards of protein products for you.
- We've changed what value for money can mean to you.
- We've changed how products are formulated with you in mind.
- We've changed how products are produced providing you with both performance and health.
- We've changed the type of guarantee that you can expect.
- We're totally committed to make changes to your physique and health more achievable.

Find out more about these changes at:

www.reflex-nutrition.com

Please visit & join our Facebook page at Reflex Nutrition Ltd

@ReflexNutrition

reflex®
Tomorrow's Nutrition Today™

● STARTING TRAINING

SYNTHETIC TRACK

If you're lucky enough to live within distance of a synthetic track (almost all British tracks are now made of modern synthetic materials), they can provide a useful alternative to road and an excellent surface for structured running sessions. They can be extremely versatile — and not just for sprinters. You might need to join the local running club, although some tracks offer pay-as-you-go usage.

Pros: Synthetic tracks provide a reasonably forgiving surface (depending on what they're laid on) and, being exactly 400 metres around, make measuring distances and timing sessions easy.

Cons: With two long curves on every lap, ankles, knees and hips are put under more stress than usual. You would be unlikely to run a long steady on a track.

Conclusion: Tracks are ideal for speedwork, but you have to be dedicated to use them for anything else.

SAND

I used to have a running buddy who, religiously, once a week drove to Camber Sands to do a steady run — in his bare feet. Sand is one of nature's most forgiving surfaces. If it's dry and deep, you can give your calf muscles a great low-impact work-out. If you want a faster workout, run on the harder-packed stuff or use the natural dunes.

Pros: Sand gives an opportunity to run barefoot in a pleasant environment. Running through dunes provides good resistance training and strengthens the legs.

Cons: Despite being great for building leg strength, soft sand means a higher risk of Achilles injury. Also, though the sand is firmer at the water's edge, the tilt of the surface puts uneven stresses on the body. Shoes may also be needed, given the litter on many of Britain's beaches.

Conclusion: Flat, firm sand can be a near-perfect running surface, but most beaches have cambers and any uneven footing can overstress muscles. Best in limited doses.

The Ultimate Guide to Marathon Running

SNOW

There's nothing more spectacular than running on 'virgin' snow — being the first person to make an imprint on the white blanket that covers local fields can be deeply satisfying. Unfortunately, if you live in Britain, you won't have many opportunities to run on snow. That's not necessarily a bad thing: running on snow is hard work and there are the hidden dangers of ice to contend with — as well as wet, cold feet.

Pros: Snow can convert a drab park into a winter wonderland. It also forces a slow pace, which is excellent for muscles recovering from injury.

Cons: Once broken, snow can be slippery, while slush, ice and frozen footprints make the going unpredictable. Snow can hide dangerous objects and cause muscle fatigue, and, as well as increasing your risk of injury, it's bad for your shoes.

Conclusion: Initially a pleasant change, but the feeling doesn't usually last.

ASPHALT

Asphalt is the mixture of gravel, tar and crushed rock that makes up 95% of Britain's roads. It isn't the softest surface around, but it's difficult to avoid — and it's better than concrete.

Pros: Asphalt is one of the fastest surfaces you can find, it's easy to measure distances on and simple to keep up a steady rhythm. While it's rather solid, it's a predictable, even surface that puts less strain on the Achilles tendon than softer or uneven terrains.

Cons: You face cambers, pot-holes, traffic and a pretty unforgiving surface that does put a strain on the body.

Conclusion: Though it's a hard surface to run on, asphalt is also one that's hard to stay away from. If you intend to race on it, some training on it is advisable.

CONCRETE

Concrete is primarily made up of cement (crushed rock) and it's what most pavements and 5% of roads are constructed from. It delivers the most shock of any surface to a runner's legs.

Pros: Concrete surfaces tend to be easily accessible and very flat, and, if you stick to pavements, you can avoid traffic. You can also use the lamp-posts for various rep sessions.

Cons: The combination of a hard surface (reckoned to be 10 times as hard as asphalt), kerbs and the need to sidestep pedestrians can lead to any number of injuries.

Conclusion: City dwellers probably have little choice but to do a large proportion of their running on concrete. If you get the slightest opportunity, though, look for softer surfaces.

The Ultimate Guide to Marathon Running

● STARTING TRAINING

Treadmill running

If you don't want to run outside, a treadmill can provide a useful alternative

INGRID KRISTIANSEN used one in the build up to her 1985 marathon world record; Liz McColgan used to stare at a blue dot on the wall for two hours while running on hers; and millions of people use them in gyms around the country every day.

Many running purists turn their noses up at treadmills, citing the benefits of exercising in the great outdoors as the main added benefit of running. But they're missing a trick.

Cyclists have been using stationary bikes as part of their structured training programmes for years and, considering the inclement nature of the British weather, you can hardly blame them.

So, if it works for cyclists, shouldn't indoor training work for runners?

There are few disadvantages of training on a treadmill - after all, a calorie burned is a calorie burned whatever the activity.

But, while the physiological benefits might be the same, treadmill running has added benefits that its outdoor equivalent can't offer.

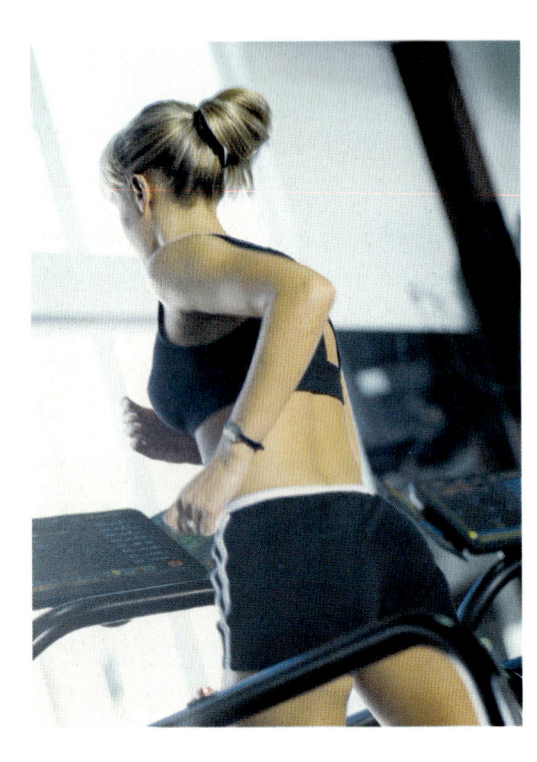

The Ultimate Guide to Marathon Running

Examples of TREADMILL RUNNING

■ **Fartlek** - or mixed interval running - is a great idea for indoor workouts because it really helps break up the monotony and get the person's mind off the fact that they aren't actually moving anywhere.

■ **Tempo runs** - where you warm up for five minutes and then run at a speed at which talking is uncomfortable (not that there will be anyone to talk to) for 15-20 minutes.

■ **Hills** - many treadmills come equipped with an incline function, enabling you to mimic the effects of running up a hill. Do some short, sharp repetitions and feel your legs burn!

■ **Interval sessions** - the classic runner's tool, but easily controlled on a treadmill. Choose your speed and then run to a set time or distance. This is great for building speed endurance and should result in you running faster back on terra firma.

■ **LSD (long, slow, distance)** - great for building stamina (mental as well as physical), but can be prone to induce boredom. Stick on your MP3 player and hum while you run.

GREAT FOR BEGINNERS

FOR A start, treadmill running is ideal for beginners. It's easy to feel a bit intimidated if you're new to the sport or talking to more experienced runners (if there's one thing runners love to do, it's talk about how much training they're doing!).

Running on a treadmill gives beginners a great place to start so they can build confidence. Anyone new to the sport will start with a mixture of walking and running: a treadmill is ideal for this because the speed can be easily adjusted to match the effort. Treadmills are also in 'safe' environments, which for women new to running can be an excellent motivator. Dark nights and lousy weather are not great inspirations without the worry of 'unsavoury' elements.

Today's treadmills allow you to jog, run, sprint, climb hills or even resistance train by easily and accurately varying grade and speed. Many come with pre-programmed training schedules or with add-ons that enable you to customise your workouts. Treadmill workouts have an unlimited number of possible combinations of speed, distance and incline. You are able to design a run that will provide you with the exact training that you desire.

Another advantage of treadmills is that they are more forgiving then the road because they absorb shock better and are less likely than road running to cause impact injuries. This will help you to run as efficiently as possible and can be a great help to someone coming back from an injury or a beginner starting out in the sport.

Since running on the treadmill is usually a solitary activity, it helps build self-motivation and commitment. Running and maintaining your pace on the treadmill builds a mental toughness that can help you in your races and outside training runs.

However, a common criticism of treadmills is that runners find them boring (running in one spot with no change of scenery is not particularly stimulating). This is why gyms tend to blast out brash dance music or have treadmills fitted with mini TVs.

Running on a treadmill without these external stimuli may build mental toughness, but it can also cause people to shorten sessions or avoid treadmills altogether (it can also get quite hot: try using a treadmill after someone's pushed themselves to the limit and you'll see what I mean). One way to keep your treadmill running fresh is to vary your workouts so that you're not just running at one speed for a given length of time.

Safety first

Treadmill training is a safe activity, but a brief lapse in concentration can cause a mishap. so follow the treadmill safety checklist below before you begin

Emergency stop - Many models of treadmill have a safety cord that you can clip onto your clothing. The opposite end of the cord is then attached to the emergency stop button and will shut down the machine if you move too far away from the front.

Stop and start - Never get on or off a treadmill when the belt is moving. Always wait for the belt to come to a halt before dismounting and, similarly, never jump onto a moving treadmill - unless you want to come flying off the back.

Keep in control of your exercise - For a smooth running action, try to stay in the middle of the belt, rather than bunched up at the front by the control console. However, always make sure that you can reach the controls without any difficulty.

Keep your exercise - focus Walking, jogging and running are all great ways to unwind, but - unlike when you train outdoors - you still need to maintain your concentration so that you don't slip. If you enjoy listening to your favourite sounds while you train, make sure you don't get lost in the music!

Know your running pace - Speed sessions on a treadmill can be very effective, but make sure that the speed you key in to the machine is within your capabilities for the duration of your session, so that you don't risk coming off the back.

The Ultimate Guide to Marathon Running

● STARTING TRAINING

Advantages

BEATING THE WEATHER
Sometimes, when the wind is howling or the snow or rain is plummeting down, you'd rather be anywhere than outside. This is when a treadmill comes in handy: it takes the weather out of the equation. On more than one occasion this winter, I've climbed onto my treadmill, ramped up the speed and elevation, and happily completed a session without getting pneumonia. I'm not averse to running in the rain or snow, but, sometimes, you've got to take the sensible option. No one's going to thank you if you slip on the ice or break your ankle on cracked pavement.

SPEED WORK
To get the most out of your interval training, you need to be doing the reps at a precise speed and distance (this is why many people use a running track). However, it can be hard for most runners to accurately judge pace while training at a track and this becomes even more difficult when training on the open road (unless you've got a handy GPS watch). Using a treadmill, you'll know exactly how far and fast you're going.

EASY RUNS
Recovery is an important part of training and, yet, many runners just don't like running slowly. Easy runs are necessary to allow your muscles to recover from hard, intense or long running sessions, but it can be very difficult to run at a pace easy enough to allow for muscle recovery. It can feel very slow and, therefore, many runners have a tendency to perform their easy runs at too fast a pace. The treadmill fixes this problem. Once you determine your easy pace, it is a simple matter to set the treadmill at that pace and jump on. As long as you don't crank up the pace, you'll complete your easy run and feel the benefits.

HILL TRAINING
Some people are blessed with a multitude of hills in their local environment; for others, finding a hill close to home can be something of a challenge. Using a treadmill solves all that. Most treadmills will elevate the running belt from 1% to 12%: some even have a decline function. Obviously, what goes up comes down, so if you want to guarantee a flat run, then a treadmill is the perfect solution.

Disadvantages

The treadmill provides many benefits, but it is not perfect. Along with its many advantages, the machine does have some disadvantages.

SPECIFICITY
One of the 'laws' of training is the law of specificity. This simply means that your training should be as specific as possible to your training goal. In other words, your training should match your goal as closely as possible. Treadmill training has been proven, in scientific studies, to have very similar physiological effects to outside or free-range running. In simpler terms, treadmill training gives you very similar training benefits when compared to free-range running. However, even though the physiological effects are very similar, it is not specifically the same as running outside.

LACK OF WIND RESISTANCE
When running on a treadmill, you are obviously running in situ. When you run outside, you are running through the molecules of the air, which create resistance. The faster you run, the more of an effect the air resistance has on you. Studies have estimated that air resistance creates an increase in your running workload of between 2% and 10%, depending upon your running speed. The faster you run, the more of an effect the wind resistance has. You can compensate for the wind resistance by elevating the treadmill by 1% or 2%.

RUNNING SURFACE
The even and soft surface of a treadmill is an advantage in many ways, particularly if you're coming back from injury, but it does present one major disadvantage. When running outside, you encounter uneven surfaces, stones, soft areas, hard areas, dry areas, wet areas and various combinations of these surfaces. The challenge of running over these surfaces improves your proprioception or the ability of your neuromuscular system to correct for the effect these surfaces have on your muscles and the position of your body parts and joints. This is critical to runners because it affects balance, power and running economy. Running on a treadmill removes this important part of training.

OTHER TREADMILL TIPS

■ Use a heart-rate monitor. Many treadmills allow you to sync your HRM with the machine itself, giving you heart-rate readings on the display panel. By using one you can eliminate 'junk training' and get fitter faster. The monitor allows you to maximise your efforts by guiding your intensity so that you work out in the zone that you want to be in, helping you to get results faster.

■ Drink. Be sure to hydrate lots while working out on a treadmill. You can lose even more water running on a treadmill than you would if you were running outside. This is because of the lack of air resistance to help to keep you cool. Just a 1% loss in water can lead to a noticeable decline in performance.

■ Towel off. Some treadmills have a small fan in their display unit, but, even with this, you'll get hot. Take a towel so that you remove excess sweat and prevent it dripping all over your unit.

The Ultimate Guide to Marathon Running

Training terms explained

LONG SLOW DISTANCE

DEFINITION: Long slow distance (often called LSD) is both a phrase commonly used to describe a training method for running or cycling and a way of running for non-competitive runners, particularly those preparing to finish their first marathon

Long slow distance running was invented - or at least promoted - as a training method by Joe Henderson in his book published in 1969. Henderson, a prolific writer of running articles since 1960, saw his approach as providing an alternative to the dominant training method for distance running, which he called the 'PTA school of running - the pain, torture, and agony' approach.

Long slow distance running is exactly that: a typical 5k runner might do 8 to 10 miles LSD, while a marathoner might run 20 or more miles. LSD runs are typically done at an easy pace, the kind of pace at which having a conversation is easy and, typically, 1-3 minutes per mile slower than a runner's 10k pace.

> *LSD isn't just a training method. It's a whole way of looking at the sport. Those who employ it are saying running is fun: all running, not just the competitive part which yields rewards*
> — Joe Henderson

The upside
1. Builds blood volume and increases muscle strength, endurance and aerobic fitness.
2. Better use of the body's fat energy stores and, therefore, greater potential for weight loss.
3. Less possibility of injury (providing other variables, such as correct footwear, are adhered to).
4. Less stress on the body.
5. More sociable.

The downside
1. It takes an awful long time to do.
2. Can be difficult to find interesting routes for runs of more than 90 minutes (and there is a greater possibility of getting lost).
3. Danger of becoming stuck at one pace.
4. Can lead to other biomechanical problems because of the time spent on your feet.

FARTLEK

DEFINITION: Fartlek, which means 'speed play' in Swedish, is a form of conditioning that puts stress mainly on the aerobic energy system due to the continuous nature of the exercise. The difference between this type of training and continuous training is that the intensity or speed of the exercise varies, meaning that aerobic and anaerobic systems can be put under stress. Most fartlek sessions last a minimum of 45 minutes and can vary from aerobic walking to anaerobic sprinting. It's fun and varied.Origins

Fartlek training was developed in the 1930s by Swedish coach Gösta Holmér and has been adopted by many physiologists since. It was designed for the downtrodden Swedish cross-country teams that had been thrashed throughout the 1920s by Paavo Nurmi and the Finns. Holmér's plan used a faster-than-race pace and concentrated on both speed and endurance training.

How do you do it?

Sessions should be at an intensity that causes the athlete to work at 60-80% of his or her maximum heart rate (estimated at 220 minus age). This should mean that the body will not experience too much discomfort while exercising. A runner should also include a good warm-up at the beginning of the session and a cool-down at the end of the session to improve performance and to decrease the chances of injury. It should be harder than a steady run.

The Ultimate Guide to Marathon Running

STARTING TRAINING

AN EXAMPLE FARTLEK SESSION

- Warm up: easy running for 5 to 10 minutes.

- Steady, hard speed for 1.5-2km; like a long repetition.

- Recovery: rapid walking for about 5 minutes.

- Start of speed work: easy running interspersed with sprints of about 50-60m, repeated until a little tired.

- Easy running with three or four quick steps now and then (simulating suddenly speeding up to avoid being overtaken by another runner).

- Full speed uphill for 175-200m.

- Fast pace for 1 minute.

- The whole routine is then repeated until the total time prescribed on the training schedule has elapsed.

ADVANTAGES OF FARTLEK

1. You make it what you want: you decide the number or length of repetitions and the variety of terrain

2. It improves aerobic capacity by increasing your lactic threshold (the point at which your body starts producing significant levels of lactic acid because of anaerobic respiration).

3. Can be done anywhere, such as the park.

4. It doesn't take huge amounts of time to do and is more interesting than steady-state running.

5. Easy on the mind because there are no strict time or distance goals.

HILLS

DEFINITION: It doesn't take a genius to work out that hill running means exactly that: running uphill (or occasionally down) in a structured training session that includes either repetitions broken by a recovery or a consistent effort of running up and down over a given period of time (say, 25 minutes).

Types of hill training

Not all hills are the same (e.g. in inclination or length), so the benefits of short, medium and long hills are quite different, and can be used at different times of the year.

Short hills

A short hill is one that takes no more that 30 seconds to run up and has an inclination of between 5 and 15 degrees. When running up this kind of hill, you should focus on a running technique that has vigorous arm drive and high knee lift, with the hips kept high, so you are 'running tall', not leaning forwards.

The session is anaerobic (it puts you into oxygen debt), so the recovery time can be long - a walk back down the hill or a slow jog of 60-90 seconds. How much you do depends on how fit you are and what you're looking to achieve. Be warned: these kinds of hills can be painful - even more so 24-28 hours after you've done the session!

Medium hills

A medium hill is one that takes between 30-90 seconds to run up. This length of hill combines the benefits of the short hills with the stresses on muscular endurance and tolerance of lactic acid. Use a hill at a gradient of around 10%, so that you can run at something near race pace.

These kinds of hills are the bread and butter of any runner's training programme. The session is over relatively quickly and the 'return' you get in terms of training effect is fantastic. Yes, they may still hurt, but this pain is more than offset by the gain.

Start with 6-8 repetitions with a slow jog/walk back down recovery. As the weeks progress, increase the number of repetitions and decrease the time it takes to get back down. Be vigilant - it's very easy to lose seconds by stopping for a breather at the top before you start your 'recovery'. This is cheating!

Work on technique: you don't have to go for the same kind of arms pumping and high knee lift of the short hills. Instead, try to lengthen your stride and dig in when you feel the hill really start to 'bite'. Keep a high cadence and push on through the pain.

Long hills

A long hill is one that takes anything from 90 seconds to three minutes plus. This is similar to a long speed-endurance session, although you're going uphill.

It can be difficult to find a hill of this length that has a consistent gradient: don't worry too much. If the hill levels out at the top, you'll be able to alter your stride length to finish; if it's easier in the middle, speed up before attacking the next rise.

Many running groups use long hills as a staple of winter marathon training. This is partly because of the excellent training effect they offer, but also because of the social aspect. You can regroup at the top and run back down together or you can pick up the slower runners on the way back down.

Hills are speed work in disguise Frank Shorter, American distance legend

INTERVALS

DEFINITION: Interval training is broadly defined as repetitions of high-speed/intensity work followed by periods (the periods that are the actual intervals) of rest or low activity.

Interval training is the one of the most important (if not the most important) keys to running faster. Running long distances alone does not develop the explosive energy systems to consistently improve your speed.

There are many different types of interval training. The type of interval training that is best for you depends on the distance of the race you are running.

Types of Intervals

Intervals fall into two main camps: longer and less intense; shorter and faster.

Longer intervals.
such as mile or 3k repeats, are used to help prepare runners for long races such as the marathon or half marathon. They are done at slightly faster than race pace and usually need a recovery of between one to two minutes.

Shorter, higher-intensity intervals
are used to help prepare you for faster, shorter races such as 5k and 10k, as well as adding some leg speed into your marathon training. These intervals could be anywhere from 60 seconds to three minutes and are done at a pace considerably than race pace and at a heart rate that is around 85-90% of maximum. More time is needed to recover between repetitions: the faster you run, the more recovery you'll need.

EXAMPLES OF INTERVAL SESSIONS

LONGER:
- 4-6 x 1 mile with 60secs recovery
- 3 x 8mins with 2mins recovery
- 3, 4, 5, 5, 4, 3mins with 90secs between reps
- 6mins, then 5 x 3mins with 60secs recovery
- 5 x 4mins with increasing recoveries (60, 70, 80, 90 seconds)

SHORTER:
- 10-12 x 60secs with 60secs recovery
- 6-10 x 2mins with 90secs recovery
- 30, 60, 90, 60, 30secs with 45secs recovery (2mins between sets)
- 2mins, 30secs x 6 (60secs recovery between each rep)
- 20 x 30secs, 100metres walk recovery

BENEFITS
1. Interval training prepares you for the sudden bursts of intense activity or stress that runners experience.
2. Interval training improves the body's ability to utilise oxygen.
3. Interval training workouts are fast. You can get the same or better benefits by doing an interval training workout that lasts a total of 4 minutes as you would with a 1-hour run at about 65% of your maximum.
4. It improves your fat-burning ability. Interval training nearly exhausts your muscles' carbohydrate reserves known as glycogen. During the hours after your workout, your body uses fat to replace the glycogen that you depleted.
5. It's incredibly versatile and can be done almost anywhere.
6. Interval training improves the efficiency of the heart.

THRESHOLD RUNNING

There's a lot of confusion about what threshold running is. Some people think it's just about running fast; others believe it's about running at certain speeds.

There is an element of truth in both of these, but threshold running is about exercising at pre-determined heart rates that are a percentage of your maximum heart rate.

The session is meant to be run as fast as possible, while remaining entirely aerobic (in other words, the body is replenished with as much oxygen as is being used during the activity - at no stage will the body go into oxygen debt). Accomplishing this is often difficult because it is not easy to tell whether you are running entirely aerobically. In fact, it can feel extremely hard, particularly if you're slightly under the weather and, consequently, struggling to reach your usual heart-rate zones.

If all that sounds too scientific, don't be alarmed. You don't need to step into a sports science lab to calculate your maximum heart rate - and, subsequently, your threshold levels (although this does produce the most accurate results). But it might be helpful to own a heart-rate monitor. These can differ significantly in price, but, at their most basic (and cheapest), they will tell you what your current heart rate is.

The Ultimate Guide to Marathon Running

STARTING TRAINING

CALCULATING HEART RATES

The easiest and best-known method to calculate your maximum heart rate (MHR) is to use the formula MHR = 220 - Age

This has, however, been superceded by a number of other formulae:

A paper by Londeree and Moeschberger (1982), from the University of Missouri-Columbia, indicates that the MHR varies mostly with age, but the relationship is not a linear one. They suggest an alternative formula of

MHR = 206.3 - (0.711 x Age)

A paper by Miller et al (1993), from Indiana University, proposed the following formula as suitable for calculating MHR:

MHR = 217 - (0.85 x Age)

Meanwhile, research carried out by scientists at John Moores University in Liverpool (UK) in 2007, reported in the Int J Sports Med 2007;24, came up with the following formulae for predicting maximum heart rates in endurance and anaerobically trained athletes:

Male athletes MHR = 202 - (0.55 x age)
Female athletes MHR = 216 - (1.09 x age)

Whichever one of these you use, you will need a figure to calculate your target threshold training zones. This can be done using the Karvonen Method, which will give you a figure for between 60-80% of MHR.

1. Find your resting heart rate as soon as you wake up

You can do this by counting your pulse for one minute while still in bed. You may average your heart rate over three mornings to obtain your average resting heart rate (RHR). Add the three readings together and divide that number by three to get the RHR. For example:
(76 + 80 + 78) / 3 = 78

2. Find heart-rate reserve

Subtract your RHR from your MHR. This is your heart-rate reserve (HRmaxRESERVE). For example:
HRmaxRESERVE = 196 - 78 = 118

3. Calculate the lower limit of your THR

Work out 60% of your HRmaxRESERVE (multiply by 0.6) and add your RHR to the answer. For example:
(118 * 0.6) + 78 = 149

4. Calculate the upper limit of your THR

Work out 80% of the HRmaxRESERVE (multiply by 0.8) and add your RHR to the answer. For example:
(118 * 0.8) + 78 = 172

5. Divide the values obtained in steps 3 and 4 by 6 to obtain your THR in beats per ten seconds

For example:
149 / 6 = 25 (lower limit)

172 / 6 = 29 (upper limit)

HEART-RATE TIPS

TIP ONE: When taking a reading for your resting heart rate, make sure you do so the morning after a day when you have rested - trying to do it the day after a hard workout can affect your results.

TIP TWO: Ensure, during your workout, that your heart rate falls within your target heart-rate zone to maximise cardiovascular fitness.

TIP THREE: A rule-of-thumb is, if you're able to chat, you're not working out hard enough. Conversely, if you're not able to catch a quick word, you're working out too hard.

TIP FOUR: One of the most common ways to take a pulse is to lightly touch the artery on the thumb-side of the wrist, using your index and middle fingers. This is called a radial pulse check.

TIP FIVE: You may also place two fingers below the jawline, along the trachea (windpipe) to feel for a pulse, again using your index and middle fingers. This is called a carotid pulse check.

TIP SIX: When taking your pulse for 10 seconds during a workout, stop exercising. Do not allow yourself to rest before taking your pulse and immediately resume exercise after the 10 seconds. Multiply by 6 and you'll have your heart rate.

Somewhere in the world someone is training when you are not. When you race him, he'll win
Tom Fleming, two-time winner, New York Marathon

The Ultimate Guide to Marathon Running

Do a 10k run

ANOTHER WAY of finding your threshold is to complete a 10km race. Often this distance is run at around the threshold heart rate. You will need to record your heart rate as often as possible and the mile splits (clearly, a heart-rate monitor is the only practical solution unless you want to stop running every five minutes). If you are fit, you will run fast and hard and achieve a constant heart rate. For those who are not so fit or start too fast the chances are you will, at some point, run above your threshold. This is usually followed by a dramatic drop in heart rate, a rise in breathing rate and a drop in pace. If you notice these signs while running, check your monitor because there is a good chance you have discovered your threshold. Remember to rest the day before and take it easy for a couple of days after.

Threshold training

HAVING DISCOVERED your threshold, it is important to work on improving it. Your heart rate should be set about 5% below your known threshold. Threshold reps can be anything from five minutes up to a sustained run of 25 minutes (unless you're an elite athlete, I wouldn't recommend anything further than that). So you might mix and match during any one week, completing a session of 4 x 5mins with a short recovery and a 20-minute continuous run. If possible, precede each threshold with an easy recovery run. It's also worth checking your threshold every eight to six weeks.

BENEFITS OF IMPROVING LACTATE THRESHOLD

- Improved speed endurance over 10km upwards
- Speeds up marathon pace.
- Stamina to run strongly towards the end of a distance event.

Some example sessions:
- 4 x 5mins with 60 secs recovery
- 3 x 6mins with 60 secs recovery
- 3 x 8mins with 90 secs recovery
- 2 x 10mins with 60 secs recovery
- 5 x 5mins with 60 secs recovery
- 1 x 20mins
- 3 x 10mins with 90 secs recovery
- 2 x 15mins with 90 secs recovery
- 1 x 25mins

The Ultimate Guide to Marathon Running

STARTING TRAINING

Recovery runs

SOME PEOPLE see recovery runs as junk mileage, but they are an important part of the training process – both mentally and physically. Some people believe the purpose of a recovery run is to allow waste products from previous sessions to be 'flushed out' of an athlete's system. This isn't very scientific, but, basically, when you hear someone refer to a recovery run, it just means a slow run (distance tends to be dictated by what level the athlete is running at) to get rid of some of the soreness and fatigue that may have accumulated in your muscles over time.

The truth is that lactic acid levels return to normal within an hour after even the toughest workouts. And lactic acid doesn't cause muscle fatigue in the first place. Also, there is no evidence that the sort of light activity that a recovery run entails promotes muscle-tissue repair, glycogen replenishment or any other physiological response that is actually relevant to muscle recovery.

The real benefit of recovery runs is that they increase your fitness - perhaps almost as much as longer, faster runs do - by challenging you to run in a pre-fatigued state (one in which you're still carrying the after-effects of the previous night's mile reps).

Evidence shows that fitness adaptations occur not so much in proportion to how much time you spend exercising, but rather in proportion to how much time you spend exercising beyond the point of initial fatigue in workouts. 'Key' workouts (runs that are challenging in their pace or duration) boost fitness by taking your body well beyond the point of initial fatigue.

Recovery workouts, on the other hand, are performed entirely in a fatigued state and, therefore, also boost fitness, despite being shorter and/or slower than key workouts.

It is, however, important to make a distinction between recovery runs and 'junk miles'. Recovery runs have a purpose: they help the body recover and set you up for the next hard session. Don't be fooled into sticking a harder steady run in between sessions: the body is not able to cope with being pushed to its limits day in, day out. At best, you will not be able to run your 'proper' hard sessions at the right level; at worst, you will over-fatigue the body and, in the most extreme cases, induce 'under performance syndrome'.

Rest is good: if it wasn't, marathon runners wouldn't bother tapering before a marathon. You won't lose any fitness by having recovery runs as part of your training programme or by following a schedule that has easy days built into it. A good friend and former international athlete used to use a 17-day cycle in which he ran 12 days hard and then five days easy, before completing the cycle again. This resulted in him producing the best results of his career - and staying healthy and injury-free.

I'm never going to run this again
Grete Waitz after the first of nine NYC Marathons

TOP TIPS FOR USING RECOVERY RUNS

TIP ONE: Whenever you run again within 24 hours of completing a key workout, the follow-up run should usually be a recovery run.

TIP TWO: Recovery runs are only necessary if you run four times a week or more.

TIP THREE: There's little point doing recovery runs during the 'build' phase of your marathon training, when much of what you will be doing will be well below threshold.

TIP FOUR: There are no rules governing the appropriate duration and pace of recovery runs (run for as long or as fast as you want so long as it's not detrimental to your next key session).

MAMMOTH'S ULTIMATE HEALTH MATTRESS

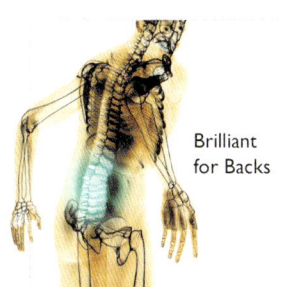

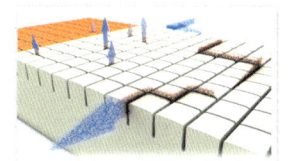

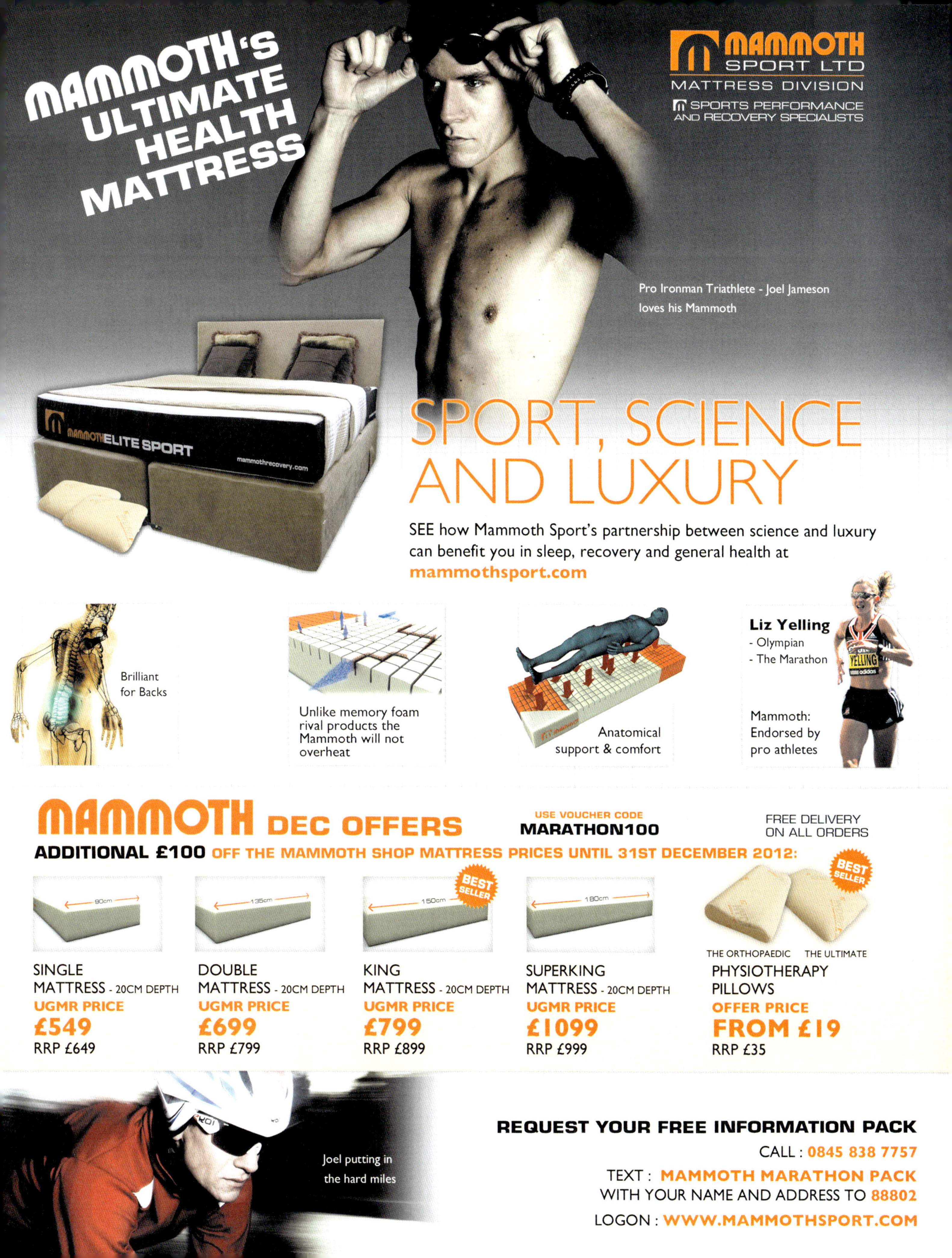

MAMMOTH SPORT LTD
MATTRESS DIVISION
SPORTS PERFORMANCE AND RECOVERY SPECIALISTS

Pro Ironman Triathlete - Joel Jameson loves his Mammoth

SPORT, SCIENCE AND LUXURY

SEE how Mammoth Sport's partnership between science and luxury can benefit you in sleep, recovery and general health at **mammothsport.com**

Brilliant for Backs

Unlike memory foam rival products the Mammoth will not overheat

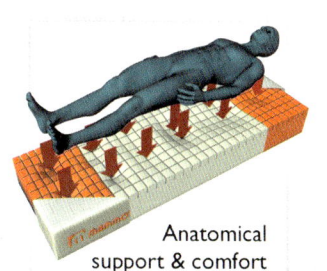

Anatomical support & comfort

Liz Yelling
- Olympian
- The Marathon

Mammoth: Endorsed by pro athletes

MAMMOTH DEC OFFERS

USE VOUCHER CODE **MARATHON100**

FREE DELIVERY ON ALL ORDERS

ADDITIONAL £100 OFF THE MAMMOTH SHOP MATTRESS PRICES UNTIL 31ST DECEMBER 2012:

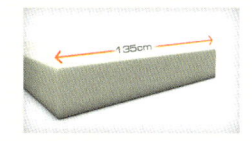

SINGLE MATTRESS - 20CM DEPTH	**DOUBLE MATTRESS** - 20CM DEPTH	**KING MATTRESS** - 20CM DEPTH	**SUPERKING MATTRESS** - 20CM DEPTH	THE ORTHOPAEDIC / THE ULTIMATE **PHYSIOTHERAPY PILLOWS**
UGMR PRICE **£549** RRP £649	UGMR PRICE **£699** RRP £799	UGMR PRICE **£799** RRP £899	UGMR PRICE **£1099** RRP £999	OFFER PRICE **FROM £19** RRP £35

(90cm / 135cm / 150cm / 180cm)
BEST SELLER

Joel putting in the hard miles

REQUEST YOUR FREE INFORMATION PACK

CALL : **0845 838 7757**

TEXT : **MAMMOTH MARATHON PACK** WITH YOUR NAME AND ADDRESS TO **88802**

LOGON : **WWW.MAMMOTHSPORT.COM**

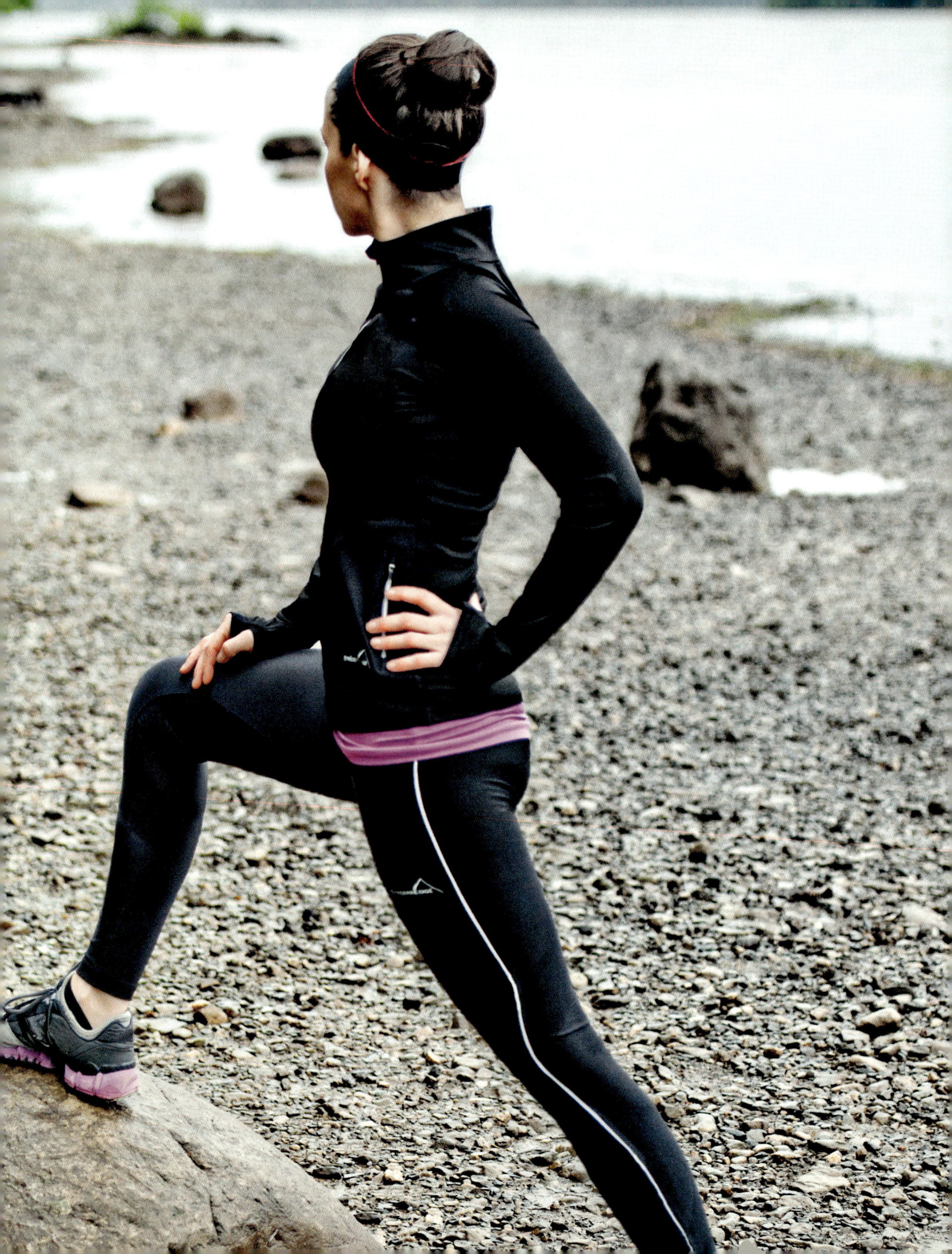

Part four

PREPARING FOR A RUN

Runners like nothing better than to swap stories about their training and - more often than not - their various injuries and ailments. This is because many runners are either inherently lazy or not aware of the benefits of stretching or conditioning - or, as is often the case, both! Runners like to run, it's that simple. While there's nothing wrong with that, if all you ever do is go out and run, without warming up or down, the chances are, you're going to pick up an injury or two. This chapter is all about the benefits of proper stretching and conditioning. There's a reason why top marathon runners incorporate stretching and conditioning into their training programmes - it's because, by doing so, they can actually spend more time training. Marathon training is about running, but it's also about making sure you get to the start line healthy. Read on to find out how.

061

STADIUMS ARE FOR SPECTATORS. WE RUNNERS HAVE NATURE AND THAT IS MUCH BETTER   JUHA VÄÄTÄINEN, FORMER EUROPEAN 10,000m CHAMPION

The Ultimate Guide to Marathon Running

● **PREPARING FOR A RUN**

Warm up ● stretching ● strength ● conditioning ● drills

GETTING READY TO RUN... AND WHAT TO DO AFTERWARDS... AND IN-BETWEEN

What do you do before and after your run? If you're anything like most runners, it'll go something like this…. Get dressed, trainers on, out of the door, bomb around your route, straight into the shower, then back to the office/pub with little thought to warming up and perhaps a cursory stretch afterwards. Sound familiar? I have to confess that, despite what I suggest to my clients and athletes, I'm sometimes guilty, too. From time to time, I do make sure I warm up properly and stretch after my session, and notice a huge difference in my running and recovery. Not really surprising.

One of the benefits of running is that it's so 'time efficient' – no extra time spent faffing about, driving to the gym or pumping up your tyres. It's one of the reasons super-busy people choose to take it up. However, if you can spend a few minutes on your warm-up routine, post-run stretching and core-stability work in between runs, you really will reap the benefits – reducing your risk of injury, improving performance and promoting recovery.

The Ultimate Guide to Marathon Running

WARMING UP

It is now universally acknowledged that stretching before a run (especially a steady-paced run) is just not necessary. Running experts suggest that it can be unhelpful at best and harmful at worst. Stretching should be done when your muscles are 'warmed' up with increased blood flow, so stretching cold, tight muscles (i.e. before a run) is not a great idea.

Many running coaches suggest jogging for five minutes or so, then stopping to stretch when your muscles are warm before going onto your main run. This can be beneficial if you have tight spots or 'niggles' that you can stretch out 'on the run', but perhaps not a realistic option when you're pressed for time or when you're out on a club run.

There is one major exception, however. If you're going to be doing some fast efforts, track work, sprinting hills or a race (less than a half marathon), stretching AFTER a warm-up jog, but BEFORE your main session/race, is vital and could help your performance and reduce the risk of muscle tears.

IF PRE-RUN STRETCHING IS A NO-NO, HOW DO YOU WARM UP?

The purpose of warming up, prior to a run, is to gradually increase your core temperature, slowly increase the blood flow to the muscles that need it (i.e. heart, lungs and working muscles) and to prepare your body for some hard work.

Taking your joints and muscles through a specific range of movement - i.e. ones akin to running - is called dynamic stretching because you don't hold the stretch, just mobilise the joints and muscles.

Two or three minutes spent doing this before breaking into an easy warm-up jog will pay dividends. You'll notice that some upper-body movements are also included in this routine. This helps to get rid of all that 'deskbound' tension in your upper body and helps you to move more freely.

The Ultimate Guide to Marathon Running

● PREPARING **FOR A RUN**

WARM UP ROUTINE

Go through each movement 8-10 times, moving slowly, steadily and breathing normally.

1. Neck Roll
Take your ear down to your shoulder, then roll your chin down to your chest and up to the other side.

2. Shoulder Roll
Lift your shoulders to your ears, keeping your hands low, rolling the shoulders round and back.

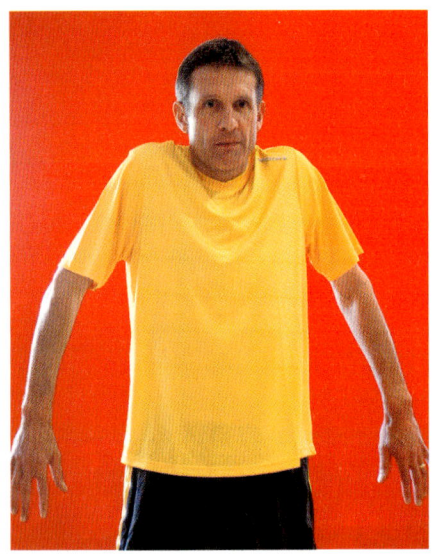

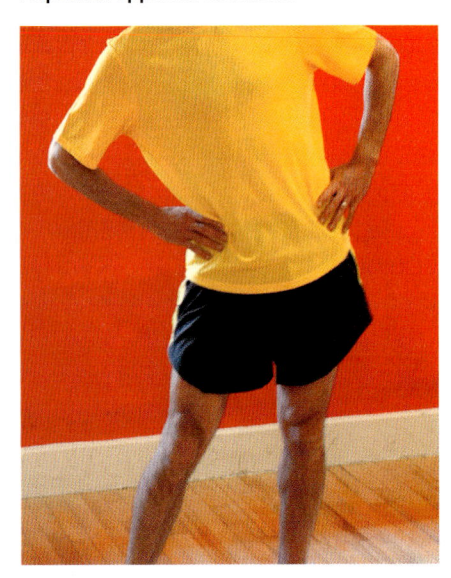

5. Leg Swing
With hands on hips for balance, swing one leg forwards and then backwards – TRY NOT TO ARCH THE LOWER BACK.

3. Knee lift
Pull your knee up to your chest, pause, circle your ankle then repeat on the other side. FILLFILLFILL

4. Hip Roll
With hands on hips and knees slightly bent, make a large circle with your hips. Repeat in opposite direction.

TOP TIP: Never start your run up a steep hill, you could risk injury as you won't be warmed up enough. Find a flatter start to your run or walk up the hill as part of your warm-up.

The Ultimate Guide to Marathon Running

6
UPPER-BODY ROTATIONS
With hands clasped and elbows wide at shoulder height, rotate slowly to each side, keeping hips forwards. Look over your shoulder. repeat to other side.

Once you've gone through your warm-up routine, spend 2-3 minutes walking briskly to raise your heart-rate and body temperature before easing into your normal pace. Try it and see if you can feel the difference. Hopefully, you'll feel as if you are running more freely and with less tension in your body.

If you're doing a speed session, fast repeats or a race (half-marathon or less), after a five-minute warm up, go through some of the stretches outlined in the 'stretching' section.

● PREPARING **FOR A RUN**

STRETCHING ON THE RUN

Contrary to popular belief, it's perfectly OK to stop and stretch during a run if you need to. If you feel a tight spot or a niggle, don't just ignore it. Stop, give it a stretch and it'll likely feel a lot better. You can use a tree, bench, lamppost, kerb or anything else you happen to find along the way.

1. Kerb Calf Stretch

Use a kerb or solid edge with something (like a lamppost) to hold onto for balance. With one foot fully on the kerb, drop one heel off the edge until you feel a nice stretch. Hold (don't bounce) for 20 seconds or so and repeat on the other leg.

2. Piriformis

Stretching your piriformis and glute muscles on a run can be tricky, but, because many runners suffer from tightness in this area, it's useful to know how to do it if you're warming up for a race or if the muscles feel tight.

The standard piriformis stretch is on page 71, but, when you're out and about, lying on your back may not be practical. There are two alternatives, both of which are outlined below.

Option 1: Sit down on the floor (find a dry grassy area) with both legs out in front. Cross your left leg over the right with the left knee bent. Put your right elbow over your bent left knee and twist to the left, pushing your left knee across your body with your right elbow.

Option 2 (not illustrated): Standing up, hold onto a post or fence. Put your left foot on your right knee with your left knee bent out to the side. Squat with your right knee until it reaches 45 degrees and push your bottom out. You should feel the stretch in your left buttock.

3. Park-Bench Hamstring

Using the seat of a park bench (or the backrest if you're very flexible), lift one leg and rest the heel on the bench, facing the leg straight on and without 'locking' either knee. Lift up out of the hips and push your chest forwards, over your leg, keeping the chin and chest lifted. You should feel the stretch in the back of your thigh (hamstring). Hold for 20 seconds - no bouncing - and repeat on other leg.

The Ultimate Guide to Marathon Running

POST-RUN STRETCHING

Stretching is probably one of the most controversial topics in running and is hotly debated by experts, coaches and runners themselves. Everyone has a different view on how to do it, when to do it or, indeed, whether you should bother at all – the reality being that most runners don't do anywhere near enough. Rather controversially, some research indicates less flexible runners are actually more efficient and have better 'running economy' – which throws a spanner in the works for the stretching advocates.

While that may be the case, tight inflexible muscles are also more prone to injury, so perhaps you shouldn't skip your stretching session just yet.

Many of us offer a bit of a lip service to stretching after a run, when things feel a bit tight or when the physio tells us to i.e. when we're injured. But the benefits of stretching properly are hugely overlooked and, while it's a bit dull, it can be the one thing you do that makes all the difference to your running.

Running makes your muscles tight, so stretching them back to their 'normal' length after a run is the main reason for a post-run stretch. In addition, stretching will help maintain your flexibility (or possibly increase it), can iron out some 'specific' areas that have become over-tight and help flush the muscles of lactic acid after training.

How to stretch correctly

If we've agreed that pre-run stretching is a no-no, but post-run stretching is important, how do you go about it, which stretches are best and how long should you hold them? There are many different theories, but the basic research and advice is still this: a simple static stretch, held for 30 seconds or so, without bouncing, is the most effective method for the vast majority of runners.

How long is long enough?

Research done by the University of Cape Town found that you gain the most flexibility by holding a stretch for 30 seconds. Stretches held for 60-90 seconds had the same benefits as the 30-second stretch. Stretches held for two minutes are less effective and 10-second stretches are worthless. So hold your stretch for anything between 20-40 seconds and they'll be the most effective and you'll gain the most benefit.

How to stretch

Stretching should not feel painful. If it does, you're likely to be pushing the stretch too far. The idea is to increase the flexibility in the muscle and get it to relax. If you push too hard, the muscle fights back and contracts. Get into the right position (see next section) and gently increase the stretch until you feel controlled discomfort in the main body of the muscle. It should feel like seven out of 10 on a scale of discomfort. Hold it for 30 seconds then slowly release. Correct alignment is really important, so use the information overleaf to help guide you into the correct position. If in doubt, seek advice from a running coach or personal trainer.

The Ultimate Guide to Marathon Running

● **PREPARING FOR A RUN**

STRETCHES FOR RUNNERS

These are a selection of classic stretches that all runners should go through, preferably just after a run, but can be done any time the muscles are warm (even after a bath). They focus on the main muscles used in running and those often prone to niggles, imbalances and tightness. If you need more specific advice, contact a physio or sports therapist for help.

Follow the stretches in this order, hold for 30 seconds, relax then swap sides.

1. Hamstring

The key to doing this one correctly is to keep your chest lifted, look forwards and push your hips down and back, as if sitting on a chair. Feet should be hip-distance apart, which helps you to balance, and rest your hands on your bent leg.

2. Quad stretch

Hold onto the laces of your shoe and pull your heel up to your bottom. Bend the leg you're standing on slightly and keep the pelvis tilting forwards. You may need to hold onto a wall for balance. Keep your upper body and shoulders relaxed.

3. Soleus/Lower Calf Stretch

A hot spot for many runners, the soleus is just below the main calf muscle and above the Achilles tendon. Don't expect to feel the 'burn' because it's quite tricky to stretch. The key to doing it correctly is to take your body weight back over the leg you're stretching and tuck your bottom under.

The Ultimate Guide to Marathon Running

4
ADDUCTOR STRETCH

You'll feel this on the inside of your thigh. Keep your toes pointing forwards and your chest and head up.
MANY RUNNERS ARE TIGHT IN THIS AREA: THIS CAN HELP.

069

5
ITB (ILIOTIBIAL BAND) STRETCH

The IT band runs from your hip down to your knee and often feels like a tight elastic band on the side of your thigh. To stretch it, try crossing your feet and pushing your hip into the wall, using your arm for support. Many runners have poor flexibility in this area, so it's worth persevering.

6. Calf stretch (Gastrocnemius)

There are two options for stretching your calf muscle here - only do one or the other. You can experiment and find the one that suits you best.

Option 1: This is more intense and gives a deeper stretch. Be careful not to slip or fall off the edge. Use a step, stair or kerb and, with the ball of your foot on the edge, simply drop your heel down. Hold on for support if you need to.

Option 2: Pushing the hips forwards and 'driving' the heel into the ground increases the stretch. Keep your head up and shoulders relaxed.

The Ultimate Guide to Marathon Running

PREPARING FOR A RUN

7. Piriformis stretch

The piriformis muscle can be problematic for runners and often gets tight. There are, again, two options.

CORRECT — OPTION ONE

Option 1: This is less advanced, but if you're especially tight can be a great loosener

CORRECT — OPTION TWO

Option 2: This provides a deeper stretch for more flexible runners. Make sure you keep your back pressed into the floor and head and neck straight and relaxed.

INCORRECT

The Ultimate Guide to Marathon Running

8. Hip Flexor

Driving the hips forwards is the key to this one, making sure the front knee goes no deeper than 90 degrees. Keep your body upright and bottom tucked under. You may need to kneel on a cushion or mat - especially if you have nobbly runners' knees!

9. Glute stretch

The glutes are one of the biggest muscles in your body and deceptively used a lot in running - mainly to stabilise the pelvis. Lying on your back and pulling your knee to your chest should provide a stretch. Keep your back pushed into the floor, neck and shoulders relaxed.

10. Glute/Piriformis/Back stretch

This is a great combination stretch and feels lovely afterwards. Lifting your chest and looking over your shoulder increases the rotation. Use your opposite arm to pull your knee across to increase the stretch.

11. Chest/Shoulder stretch

Clasp your hands behind you and pull up with straight arms to feel the stretch in your chest and shoulders. Keep the pelvis strong and try not to arch your back.

12. Upper-back stretch

As runners, we get tight in the shoulders and back. Drop your head into the space between your arms and push your hands forwards. Let the pelvis relax and curve underneath, and bend your knees.

The Ultimate Guide to Marathon Running

REMEMBER
- Only stretch the muscles when they are warmed up, after a run or even, perhaps, a bath.
- Never stretch 'cold' muscles.
- Only push the stretch until you feel 'controlled discomfort', not pain.
- Hold for 20-40 seconds, then release.

ACTIVE ISOLATED STRETCHING

AIS is a stretching technique that is growing in popularity. Developed by an American kinesiologist called Aaron L. Mattes, it claims to make you more flexible than normal static stretching and many runners swear by it. Instead of holding a stretch statically for 30 seconds, the stretch is only held for two seconds – then released, but repeated 8-10 times. It's time consuming, requires concentration and is, perhaps, not for everyone, but the results are apparently quite impressive. If you want to try it, have a look at www.stretchingusa.com

STRENGTH AND CONDITIONING IN BETWEEN YOUR RUNS

NOT SO FAST! Before you skip this section on the basis that 'I'm a runner, I don't want big muscles' or 'strength training isn't important for me', think again. We're not talking about lifting heavy weights, spending hours in the gym or building muscles that Popeye would be proud of.

Instead, this section will show you how to develop a strong, balanced and injury-proof body that will keep you out on the roads for many years to come.

The majority of running injuries are the result of an imbalance in the strength or flexibility of your muscle groups (or both), not, as many people think, due to 'pounding the pavements'.

Such injuries often come about after years of poor posture, a weakness that was never quite resolved or an 'ignored' niggle - when you start running and put the body under stress, these imbalances rear their ugly heads, causing all sorts of problems.

Not all, but many, lower-leg injuries can be tracked back up to the lower back, pelvis, weak abdominals or glutes. Got a sore knee? It could be because you have a weak bottom!

Mitchell Phillips of StrideUK, a gait analysis and postural assessment clinic in Brighton, East Sussex, claims that 95% of runners have weak glute muscles, mainly because of poor posture and too much sitting down at our desks all day.

The glutes are the biggest muscles in the body and work to stabilise the pelvis when running. Phillips says: 'If the glutes aren't strong enough, other muscles will be called upon to compensate, which can then cause tightness, problems and injuries. Developing good, balanced strength can go a long way to helping avoid injuries in the first place.'

Who should do strength and conditioning work?

Basically, everyone. If you run and want to keep running, think of the following exercises as your insurance policy against injury. If you can develop a stronger, more balanced body, Phillips reckons you can significantly reduce your 'fragility' - as he puts it - to injury. Not only that, but stronger, more efficient muscles will lead to a better running style and faster race performances. Can you think of any reason not to?

see page 78 for exercises

075

The Ultimate Guide to Marathon Running

● PREPARING **FOR A RUN**

10 ESSENTIAL PRE-RUN TIPS

01 **Give every run a 'purpose' or a 'goal'.** Even if this purpose is to 'run easy' and chat to your mates – that is still a goal. Another time it may be a more focused 'interval' session, but, either way, having a goal is really important and helps give you a sense of satisfaction and achievement.

02 **Choose and plot your route.** Check out your map and think about where you're going. If you have a set route in mind you'll a) be less likely to get lost b) have less chance of cutting it short and c) especially for female runners, you can tell someone where you're going.

03 **Don't eat a large meal or heavy snack before running.** You won't have time to digest it and the energy it could provide won't reach your muscles in time. Make sure your last 'main meal' is at least 1-2 hours before your run and try a small snack (a banana) with 15-20 minutes to go. Experiment with different snacks and food timing – everyone is different.

04 **Choose the correct shoes.** Many runners have a variety of running trainers, with a different pair for road, races and trail. Know your route and your session goal, and you can pick the right shoes.

05 **Check the weather and dress accordingly.** On early morning starts or long runs, the temperature and conditions can change dramatically and you can find yourself woefully under- or over-dressed. One rule of thumb is to dress as if it's 10 degrees warmer than it really is and to start out feeling slightly 'chilly'. A lightweight, breathable gilet or waterproof that you can stash in a pocket is a great idea.

The Ultimate Guide to Marathon Running

06 **Get a running buddy.** The miles really do fly by when you catch up on all the gossip with a good mate. Arrange to meet a friend or group for an early morning or long run and you'll be much more likely to make it; especially when the rain is lashing the window and it's still dark outside!

TOP TIP – Discover for yourself when the best time to train is. If you're an early bird (or you have children who get up at an unseemly hour), make the most of your early start. Or if you can fit a run in to your lunch hour, make good use of the time. You can also run to and from work – although a shower is preferable afterwards.

07 **Lay your kit out the night before a run.** Get everything ready – kit, shoes, watch, nutrition, drinks, socks – and lay it all out next to your bed. You won't be able to step over it in the morning without putting it on.

08 If you're doing a really long run, go out the night before and stash bottles of water or sports drinks behind bushes and in trees along the way. Just remember where you've left them!

09 **Think about your post-run nutrition and get it ready before you head out of the door.** There's nothing worse than a hungry runner and an empty cupboard. Try mixing up a recovery drink and leaving it in the fridge before you go out – ready immediately when you get back.

10 **Make sure your iPod, MP3 player or Garmin is fully charged.** Finding you have a flat battery and can't listen to your motivating music will be enough to put you off your stride.

TOP TIP – Use one of the online mapping software programmes to plot run routes from your home or office. Print them off and keep in a file – you can then refer to them, choose your route and even keep track of your best times. You can set up a variety of short, long, on or off-road options. www.mapmyrun.com is one to try.

The Ultimate Guide to Marathon Running

● PREPARING **FOR A RUN**

What to do and how to do them?

These simple exercises will only take 15-20 minutes and can be done 2-3 times per week. They focus on strengthening and 'firing up' the main muscle groups that are important for runners - namely the quads, glutes, hamstrings, lower back and core stability muscles of the stomach.

We have kept them simple, basic and easy, which should appeal to busy runners with little time to spare. If you have more specific needs, contact a sports therapist or personal trainer for advice on correct alignment and additional exercises.

Do these exercises in the following order, moving steadily and slowly. Do not rush or jerk the movements and don't forget to breathe.

START POSITION

LUNGE POSITION

1. The Lunge - do 15 on each leg
Very simple, but very effective. Works the quads, glutes, calves and hamstrings all at the same time. Feet should be hip-distance apart, hands on hips for balance or hold on to a chair or wall. Start position is with feet in a 'split' stance as in photo 1 - up on your toes at the back and with heel firmly planted on the front foot. Lower yourself until your front knee is at 90 degrees, then push back up to start position. Look straight ahead and keep your bottom tucked under with chest lifted - keep most of your weight over the back leg.

The Ultimate Guide to Marathon Running

2. Basic Squat
15-20 in total

Start by standing upright with feet at hip-distance apart. Imagine that you are sitting down onto a chair, so aim your hips down and backwards as you squat. As you squat, lift your arms. Keep your knees in line with your toes and heels firmly pushed into the floor. To progress this you can hold the squat position for a count of five – keep breathing.

3. Step up and lift – 15 on each leg

Using a step or bench, step up then drive the other leg through and up into a knee lift. Keep your head up and look straight ahead. Step back down and repeat on the same leg. To progress this you can hold dumbbells in your hands to add extra weight.

The Ultimate Guide to Marathon Running

PREPARING FOR A RUN

4
SINGLE-LEG SQUAT —
Do 10 on each leg

Stand on one leg with the other bent in front of you. Bend the knee of the leg you are standing on to lower yourself into a squat position. Do not let the knee drop inwards - keep the knee in line with your thigh. Keep your head up and hands on your hips or hold on to something for balance. Hold for a count of five and repeat.

5. Press Up – do 15-20 in total

Works the core muscles and upper body, which is vital for runners who often have little strength in their arms. Make sure the hands are wider than the shoulders. Lower the chest (not your face) to the floor between your hands, and think about 'pinching' the shoulder blades together, which opens up the chest. Keep the back and stomach strong and push back up to the starting position. Many runners have little upper-body strength, so try doing the press up on your knees rather than toes to start with. Progress to your toes as you build up strength. It's better to do it correctly, than persist with wrong technique.

6. THE PLANK – HOLD FOR 20-30 SECONDS, BUILDING UP TO 2 MINUTES

One of the most effective 'core stability' exercises there is. Do this correctly by ensuring your elbows are under your shoulders and imagine a straight line from the tip of your head through your back to your heels. Keep your upper body relaxed and shoulder blades drawn down and back. Keep your bottom in line with your back – don't sag or push it up in the air. If you start to shake, lower down and repeat for a shorter time. Start on your knees, then progress to the more advanced position on your toes.

The Ultimate Guide to Marathon Running

PREPARING FOR A RUN

7. Side Plank - hold for 30-45 seconds on each side
Keeping the elbow under the shoulder is key with this one. Imagine a straight line from the tip of your head, down through your back and to your heels, and that you have a wall behind you.

8. Heel Drops (Above) - do 10 in total, very, very slowly
Push the lower back into the floor and maintain that feeling throughout. Slowly lower ONE heel down to the floor keeping the knee angle at 90 degrees. As your heel goes down, your back will want to lift - your job is to keep it pushed down and keep breathing. Slowly bring your leg back up to the start position and repeat with the other leg. The slower the better.

9. Basic Crunch (Right) - 15-20 done slowly
Very simple, but easy to do incorrectly. Keep the back pushed into the floor and elbows back. Think about lifting your chest up (imagine a piece of string is pulling you towards the ceiling) and use your hands to support the weight of your head - try not to pull. Keep breathing throughout.

The Ultimate Guide to Marathon Running

Order your print or digital MagBook at **magbooks.com** or call **0844 844 0053**

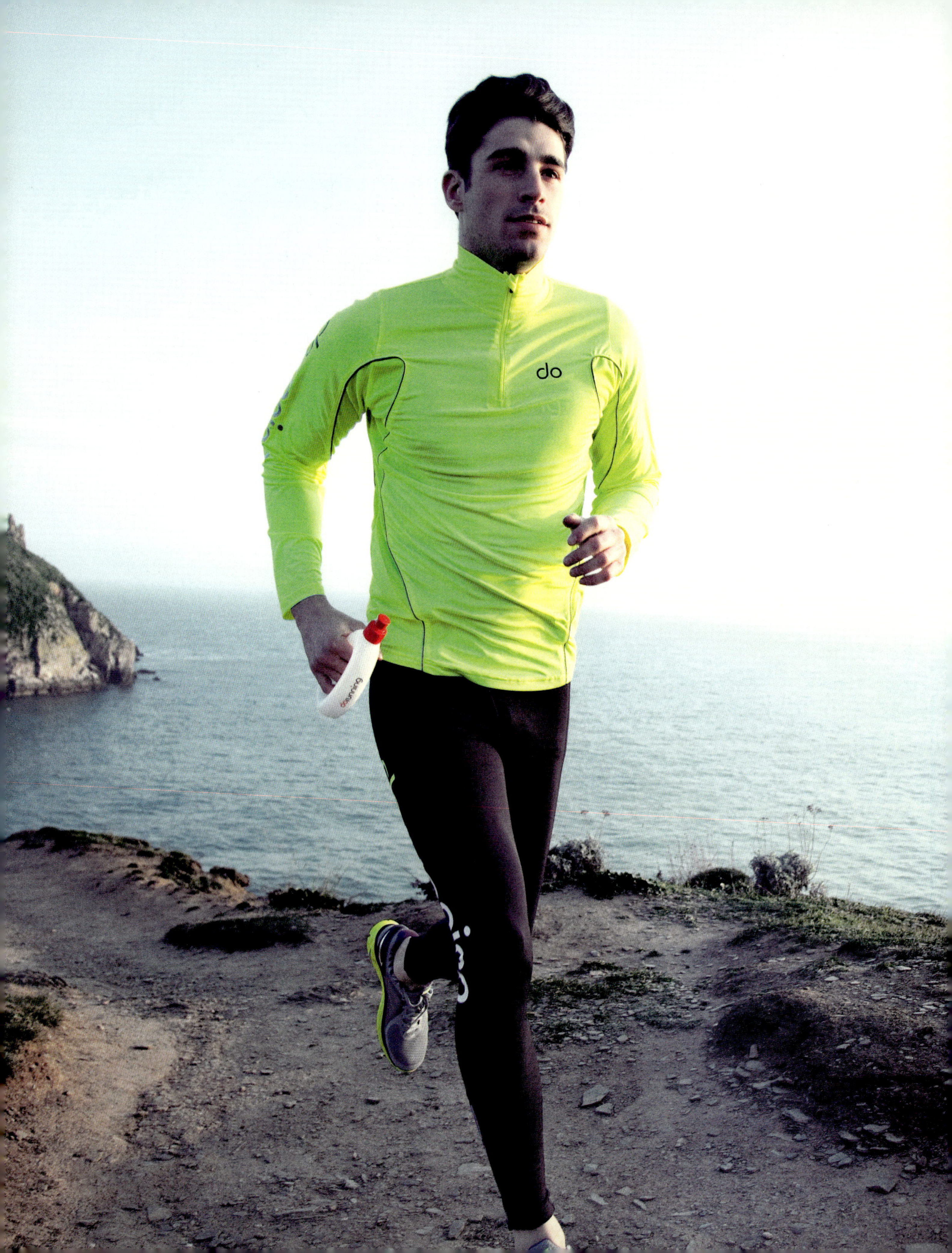
do

Part five

MARATHON NUTRITION

You are what you eat: at least that's what dieticians and nutrition experts would have us believe. And, up to a point, they're right. The growth in awareness of proper nutrition, spearheaded by the likes of Jamie Oliver and the Government's health eating agenda, have put food firmly at the forefront. By choosing to run, you've already decided that you want to be healthy, so you might be forgiven for thinking that diet isn't important. You would, of course, be wrong. If you want to run well, you should also eat well: it's simple. Marathon training should not be done on a diet of chocolate bars and fizzy drinks. Nor is running carte blanche to eat what you like, when you like. Training for a marathon is all about striking the right balance. You don't need to live like a monk, but you should think carefully about your body's nutrition. This chapter looks at the importance of proper nutrition for marathon training and how you can fuel your body for a better performance.

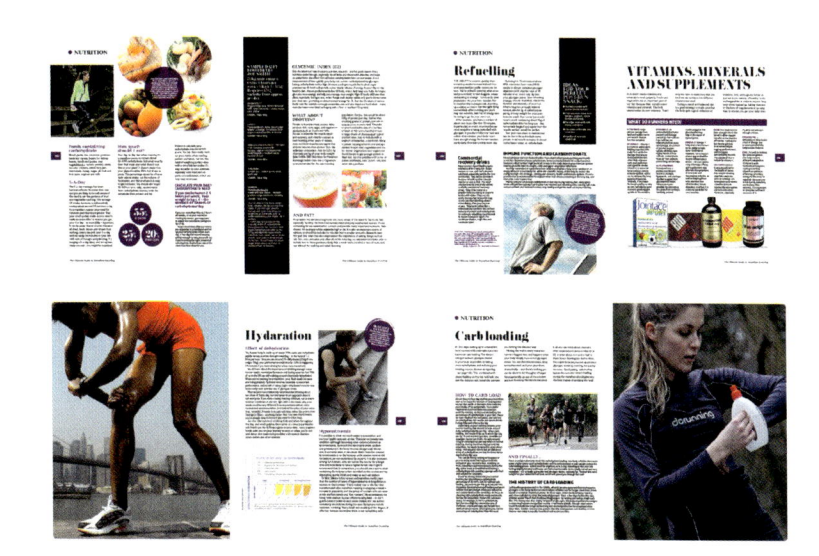

GET UP AND WALK IF YOU HAVE TO, BUT FINISH THE DAMNED RACE
RON HILL, UK RUNNING LEGEND WHO HAS COMPLETED A RUN EVERY DAY SINCE 1964

The Ultimate Guide to Marathon Running

● NUTRITION

Carbohydrate ● Gi diet ● Refuelling ● Hydration ● Fat

FOOD FOR THOUGHT

Training for a marathon is great news when it comes to nutrition – it means you can get away with eating a lot more food. In fact, you really need to. You must fuel your body with plenty of energy for all that extra running you'll be doing. But, and this is the dull bit, the type and the quality of the food you eat becomes much more important, and can be make-or-break for a good marathon experience.

Training for a marathon is not, however (and you may want to stop reading at this point), a licence to take up residence at your local chip shop or curry house. You need to put good quality fuel into your body to give it the best chance of performing at its optimum level. And don't think that nutrition is just of concern to the elite runners – it is something that can make a difference to everyone, even if you're a fun runner dressed as a fairy or the back end of a pantomime horse.

Everyone knows the benefits of eating pasta the night before a marathon. Each big city marathon has a 'pasta party' at which hungry runners get to fill their stomachs for free. But this is only a small part of the picture. As a marathon runner, you need a more in-depth understanding of what and when to eat, and why... but, more importantly, how to put it into practice many months before the race.

In this chapter, we aim to do just that. We'll look at how to optimise your diet throughout your entire marathon training programme and also show you the perfect nutrition plan for the race itself – as you'll see, they are very different things.

Ask anyone who's done a marathon and they'll tell you about the need to 'carb load' before the race. This is a well-known practice that involves increasing the intake of carbohydrate-rich foods, such as pasta, rice and bread, for a few days before the race. This process – combined with race-day fuelling – aims to provide you with enough stored energy to get you through the 26.2 miles without hitting the dreaded 'wall', the point at which you simply run out of juice. For many marathoners, this is the first time they give much thought to their diet, hoping that filling up on pasta the night before is enough. It's not. The second most important factor (after training) for a successful marathon is nutrition – and not just race-day nutrition. Start to think about what you eat NOW, months before the event, and you'll have a much happier and healthier ride to the start line – and more chance of making it to the finish.

If a marathon is a part-time interest, you will only get part-time results
Marathon legend Bill Rodgers

The Ultimate Guide to Marathon Running

IMPORTANCE OF CARBOHYDRATE

Whenever you eat foods containing carbohydrate, your body quickly converts it and stores it as 'glycogen' in the liver and muscles – rather like a fuel tank. Then, when you run, you draw upon these stores of glycogen to provide you with the extra energy for your working muscles. Having enough stored glycogen is essential for brain function and normal day-to-day energy levels, but – more importantly for you as a marathon runner – it is vital for exercise. Because you are running regularly, a topped up 'fuel tank' is crucial, which means eating a diet rich in carbohydrate and paying close attention to your pre- and post-run nutrition.

But what exactly does 'a diet rich in carbohydrate' mean and how do you go about achieving it?

BALANCE OF GOOD HEALTH

The Food Standards Agency's 'Balance of Good Health' shows the optimum diet for the vast majority of the population and especially for fit, active people. It illustrates the five basic food groups and how they should be balanced to make up a healthy diet. Many runners make the mistake of over-focusing on certain foods – eating too much or too little of one of the food groups, or eliminating another completely. The 'balance of good health' aims to show how all foods need to be included for a healthy diet and the proportions that make up the best balance. Even treats, such as chocolate, crisps and chips, should be included in small amounts – the 'balance' is the key factor in a healthy diet.

THE TWO biggest groups are 'fruit and vegetables' and 'bread, pasta, rice and other cereals'. A healthy diet for active runners is directly in line with this model, based predominantly on starches, cereals, fruit and vegetables. It is equally important, however, to include foods from the other sections (meat, fish and alternatives, dairy and fats and oils) because they all have a vital role to play, providing protein, calcium, iron and other vitamins and minerals essential for good health and performance.

Over the past decade or so, the carbohydrate message for runners has been hammered home, in some cases almost too heavily. Some runners are in danger of over-eating carbohydrate and neglecting important foods that provide muscle-repairing protein, calcium and iron.

On the other hand, the diet industry has thrust a 'negative' image onto carbohydrate, leading slimmers to cut out foods such as bread, pasta, rice and potatoes in the mistaken belief that they're fattening. It's no wonder we're confused! Hopefully, by the time you finish this chapter, you'll have a clear picture of how much carbohydrate you need to eat and how to put that into practice.

Which foods provide carbohydrate?

Sugar, also known as sucrose, fructose, maltose and lactose, is the most simple form of carbohydrate. The more complex form is starch, found in food such as bread, pasta, potatoes and rice. Many foods contain a mixture of simple and complex carbohydrate (think of a fruit bun, which mixes starch and sugar). Your training diet should be made up, predominantly, of complex carbohydrates, which fill you up, provide plenty of nutrients and fibre and give you long-lasting energy.

- We all know that fresh fruit, vegetables and juices should be eaten as part of a healthy diet

- Carbs are the foundation of any runner's diet and will help fuel you round your marathon course

- Protein is also an important nutrient for runners, helping recovery and injury prevention

- Diet is about balance, so don't rule out foods such as cake just because you think they're bad

- Dairy products, such as milk, cheese, yogurt and butter, provide minerals and good fats

087

The Ultimate Guide to Marathon Running

NUTRITION

Just because you're training for a marathon, doesn't mean you have to overload your plate with pasta, rice and bread. Get a balanced carbohydrate intake from a wide variety of sources, such as fruit, vegetables, pulses, dairy and a mix of bread, pasta, potatoes and rice.

Foods containing carbohydrate

Bread, pasta, rice, couscous, potatoes, breakfast cereals, beans (i.e. kidney beans), lentils and pulses, root vegetables (i.e. carrots, swede), cakes, biscuits, crackers, cereal bars, jam, marmalade, honey, sugar, all fruit and fruit juice, yoghurt and milk.

5-A-Day

The 5-a-day message has been hammered home for some time now and you are likely to be well aware of the need to eat five portions of fruit and vegetables each day. The average UK intake, however, is still woefully inadequate at around 2.5 portions a day. As a marathon runner, your need for nutrients and vitamins is greater than your couch-potato mate, so you need to make an extra effort to ensure you get your 5-a-day... or more (80g = a portion). It can be easier than it sounds, however: all dried, fresh, frozen and tinned fruit and veg counts towards your 5-a-day and can easily be included in your diet with a bit of thought and planning. Try keeping a 5-a-day diary and tot up how many you eat - you might be surprised

How much should I eat?

Your day-to-day diet when training for a marathon needs to contain about 55-60% carbohydrate. But what exactly does that mean and what does it look like on your plate? It doesn't mean that your plate should be 60% full of rice or pasta. The percentage should be of your daily calorie intake, not the volume of food eaten, and this is where it is easy to get confused. You should aim to get 55-60% of your daily calorie intake from carbohydrate sources, with the remainder from protein and fat.

55% CARBS

25% FAT

20% PROTEIN

It's best to calculate your carbohydrate requirement in grams. You can then easily work out your intake when reading packets and labels. Get into the habit of weighing portion sizes with a set of kitchen scales: it's easy to under- or over-estimate, especially with food such as pasta, rice and cereals, which are very easy to overeat.

CALCULATE YOUR DAILY CARBOHYDRATE NEED

If you run between 2-5 hours per week, Your weight in kg x 4 = the NUMBER OF GRAMS OF carbohydrate/day.

If you run more than this (6-7 hours per week), or as your marathon training increases, you may need to adjust the calculation (weight in kg x 5-6).

Keep a food diary (like our runner Joe, opposite) in a notebook and tot up your carbohydrate intake each day. A few days of record keeping will be enough to help you work out if you're eating the right amount of carbohydrate and to learn about the correct portion sizes for you.

The Ultimate Guide to Marathon Running

SAMPLE DAILY FOOD DIARY — JOE SMITH

75Kg male runner, trains 6 hours per week (75kg x 5 = 375g) Requires 375g carbohydrate approx per day

BREAKFAST
30g porridge oats, 300ml skimmed milk, raisins & honey, 1 glass orange juice 250ml
CARBS: Total 80g

LUNCH
Tuna sandwich, some mixed salad leaves, 1 orange, a fruit bun, fruit yoghurt and a handful of berries
CARBS: Total 90g

SNACKS THROUGHOUT THE DAY
Fruit smoothie made with banana, yoghurt and blueberries, small flapjack, 1 medium apple, handful of nuts
CARBS: Total 85g

TRAINING
13 mile run - 500ml sports drink and 1 gel
CARBS: Total 55g

DINNER
Homemade lasagne made with lean mince - medium portion. Large salad with dressing
CARBS: Total 65g

You can only do this if you weigh food, measure things out and read labels. If you don't get specific enough with your recording, you could end up drastically over- or under-estimating your intake. Try it and see.

You'll also notice that Joe has a steady intake of carbohydrate throughout the day. He starts with a good breakfast and splits up his 375g carbohydrate requirement into three main meals, two or three snacks, plus a sports drink and gel for his run. This will keep his blood-sugar levels steady and give him plenty of fuel for training.

GLYCEMIC INDEX (GI)

GI is the latest hot topic in sports nutrition research – and for good reason. It is a nutrition breakthrough, especially for athletes and those with diabetes, and helps us understand the effect that different carbohydrates have on our bodies. GI is a measurement of how quickly your body can convert carbohydrate into glycogen. Eating carbohydrate with a high GI means you'll get a quick rise in blood sugar, whereas low GI foods will provide a slow steady release of energy. In your day-to-day healthy diet, choose predominantly low GI foods, which help keep you fuller for longer, give you more energy and help you manage your weight. High GI foods still have their place, especially during a race, when things such as jelly babies and sports drinks come into their own, providing an almost instant energy fix. To find the GI values of various foods visit the website www.glycemicindex.com and also check out food labels - many manufacturers now label packaging with a 'low' or 'medium' GI symbol.

WHAT ABOUT PROTEIN?

Protein is found in meat, pulses, dairy produce, fish, nuts, eggs, and vegetarian products such as Quorn and tofu. Protein is essential for muscle repair and recovery, and vital for runners in hard training. After years of debate, most nutrition experts now agree that athletes require more protein than the sedentary population. Aim for 1.2-1.4g of protein per kg of your body weight (Jane Griffin SRD 'Nutrition for Marathon Running') rather than the 0.75g which is recommended for the non-running population. For Joe, this would be about 105g of protein per day. Rather than counting grams of protein, just aim to include some at each meal. The palm of your hand is the size of a 'portion' of meat or fish and a handful of nuts or large chunk of cheese equal typical 'portion' sizes. Aim to include milk or yoghurt at breakfast, a sandwich filling or potato topping at lunch and perhaps chicken breast with vegetables and rice for dinner. Vegetarians and vegans can find it harder to get enough protein in their diet, but it is possible with a mix of pulses and beans, nuts, Quorn, tofu and some dairy produce.

AND FAT?

As a nation, we are becoming more and more aware of the need for fat in our diet, especially 'healthy' fat from monounsaturated and polyunsaturated sources. Foods containing fat are essential for runners and provide many important nutrients. Take cheese, for example: while relatively high in fat, it is also an important source of calcium, so should be included in the diet, but in smaller amounts. Research over the past few years has also emphasised the importance of eating things such as oily fish, nuts, avocados and olive oil, while reducing our saturated fat intake. Aim to include two to three portions of oily fish a week and a handful or two of nuts, and use olive oil for cooking and salad dressing.

The Ultimate Guide to Marathon Running

● NUTRITION

Refuelling

THE ABILITY to recover quickly from a training session is essential and this is where nutrition really comes into its own. Fail to refue0l correctly after a run and you're likely to feel sluggish, weary and lacking in energy - not exactly ideal preparation for your next session. Not to mention the increased risk of picking up a cold or an injury. Eat the right thing immediately after running and you'll reap the benefits, feel full of energy and be raring to go for your next run.

After exercise, you have a window of about two hours (the first 30 minutes, in particular) in which your muscles are most receptive to being restocked with glycogen. If you don't refill your fuel tank within that window, your body won't have enough energy for its next session, particularly if you're running every day.

Running for 75 minutes at about 80% maximum heart rate (MHR) results in almost complete glycogen depletion; with shorter runs of 45 minutes or so, you'll only dip into your glycogen stores. Your refuelling strategy should, therefore, match the duration and intensity of your run. After a long run or tough interval session, aim for 1g of carbohydrate per kg of body weight for your post-exercise snack. Our runner Joe would need a snack containing about 75g of carbohydrate after his long run - the homemade flapjack and apple from the 'snacks section' would be perfect.

Your post-race snack or meal should also be low in fat and include some protein to aid muscle recovery; it should not be based solely on carbohydrate.

IDEAS FOR YOUR PERFECT POST-RUN SNACK:

- Toasted crumpet with peanut butter and jam
- Fruit smoothie made with banana, yoghurt, mixed berries and honey
- Porridge made with milk, honey and raisins
- Chocolate milkshake and a banana
- Handful of nuts and dried fruit

Commercial recovery drinks

Many runners report feeling quite nauseous after a long run, tough session or race, and can't stomach solid food, especially within the first 30 minutes. This can be a problem because refuelling after a tough session or race is vital. The ideal solution is to try one of the widely available commercial 'recovery' drinks. They often come as a powder that you mix up in a sports bottle with water. They can be easily transported in your kit-bag, so you can start drinking almost immediately after your session or race. They taste rather like a milkshake and combine the perfect balance of protein and carbohydrate for optimum refuelling. Good brands to try are Science in Sport, For Goodness Shakes, High Five and Lucozade Sport.

IMMUNE FUNCTION AND CARBOHYDRATE

It's not just your next run that will suffer if you don't refuel: you're putting your health at risk too. Depletion of your carbohydrate stores is clearly linked with a rise in a stress hormone called Cortisol. High levels of Cortisol in the body depress your immune system, leaving you wide open to coughs, colds and upper-respiratory infections.

You may have heard of a practice where athletes complete a long run or session on an empty stomach to burn body fat. While the scientific theory of this may be sound, the reality is a high-risk strategy - risking your recovery, health and immune system. It's not a practice that is recommended for anyone other than those competing at the very top, and then only under supervision.

Making sure you eat enough carbohydrate in your day-to-day training diet, using sports drinks and gels during long or particularly hard sessions and refuelling after running, will make sure you protect your immune function, stay healthy and get the most out of your training.

TOP TIP: Starting too fast in a marathon is a sure-fire way of 'hitting the wall'. Be conservative with your target time so you pace the race correctly from the start and check your watch regularly, ten seconds a mile too fast for the first 20 miles means a minute a mile slower in the last six.
— John Johnson, 65, Marathon Runner

TOP TIP: It is essential to increase your fluid intake during the 'carb loading' phase. Your body needs more water to help store glycogen, so carry a water bottle around with you everywhere in the days before the race, especially when you visit the marathon expo, where it can get hot and be dehydrating.

The Ultimate Guide to Marathon Running

VITAMINS, MINERALS AND SUPPLEMENTS

OUR BODY needs vitamins and minerals to work properly. Fruits and vegetables are an important part of our diet because they contain many vitamins and minerals. The body cannot make its own vitamins. That's why we have to make sure that the food we eat contains the different vitamins we need.

Eating a mixed and balanced diet is a good strategy to make sure that the body gets a good collection of vitamins. And, although it's better to just eat a rich variety of healthy fruits and vegetables to make sure your keep your levels topped up, taking vitamins in the form of supplements is an easy way to ensure you get your daily dose.

WHAT DO RUNNERS NEED?

VITAMIN B: helps release energy from food and makes nerve and muscle tissues function properly.

VITAMIN C: Vitamin C is a natural antioxidant, helping to protect the body from oxidative damage that occurs during exercise and other daily stresses such as air pollution and cigarette smoke. Vitamin C is also vital for ensuring a strong immune system, which can be stressed by long periods of exercise. Similarly, it increases the body's ability to take up iron, so helping good maintain good oxygen uptake to the muscles.

VITAMIN E: an antioxidant that helps prevent cell damage caused by free radicals. Free radicals are substances that cause cell damage. As a result of greater oxygen uptake athletes have higher levels of free radicals. Antioxidants 'mop up' free radicals, preventing cell damage.

GLUCOSAMINE: Glucosamine is a protein constituent found in tendons, ligaments, and cartilage. Studies suggest that glucosamine helps relieve joint pain, possibly by promoting the growth of cartilage. Similarly, animal studies suggest that glucosamine may help in the repair of injured joints.

OMEGA 3: Omega-3 fatty acid is best known for its ability to help lower cholesterol. However, for runners it is best appreciated for its anti-inflammatory action. 1 to 1 1/2 grams a day of omega-3 fatty acid supplement may alleviate the symptoms of joint pain and rheumatoid arthritis, as well as helping those with psoriasis and inflammatory bowel disorders. In effect it is a natural painkiller for sore muscles.

IRON: It is important to have enough iron in the blood to allow oxygen transfer to the muscles efficiently. Inadequate iron levels will lead to extreme fatigue, lagging performances, and increased susceptibility to colds. The uptake of iron is helped by vitamin C.

CALCIUM: Calcium is very beneficial for the health of bones. Any weight-bearing, repetitive exercise, such as running, can strengthen your bones. However overuse injuries like shin splints can turn into stress fractures, especially if you're not taking in enough calcium.

POTASSIUM: a deficiency of this causes a lack of energy due to poor control of the body's water balance

ZINC: As well as helping the immune system, zinc helps ensure efficient metabolism. It interacts with hundreds of enzymes making sure they all work at optimum efficiency, providing energy to the body as required. Because zinc is lost during sweating, particularly after exercise, it is important to consume sufficient amounts of it.

The Ultimate Guide to Marathon Running

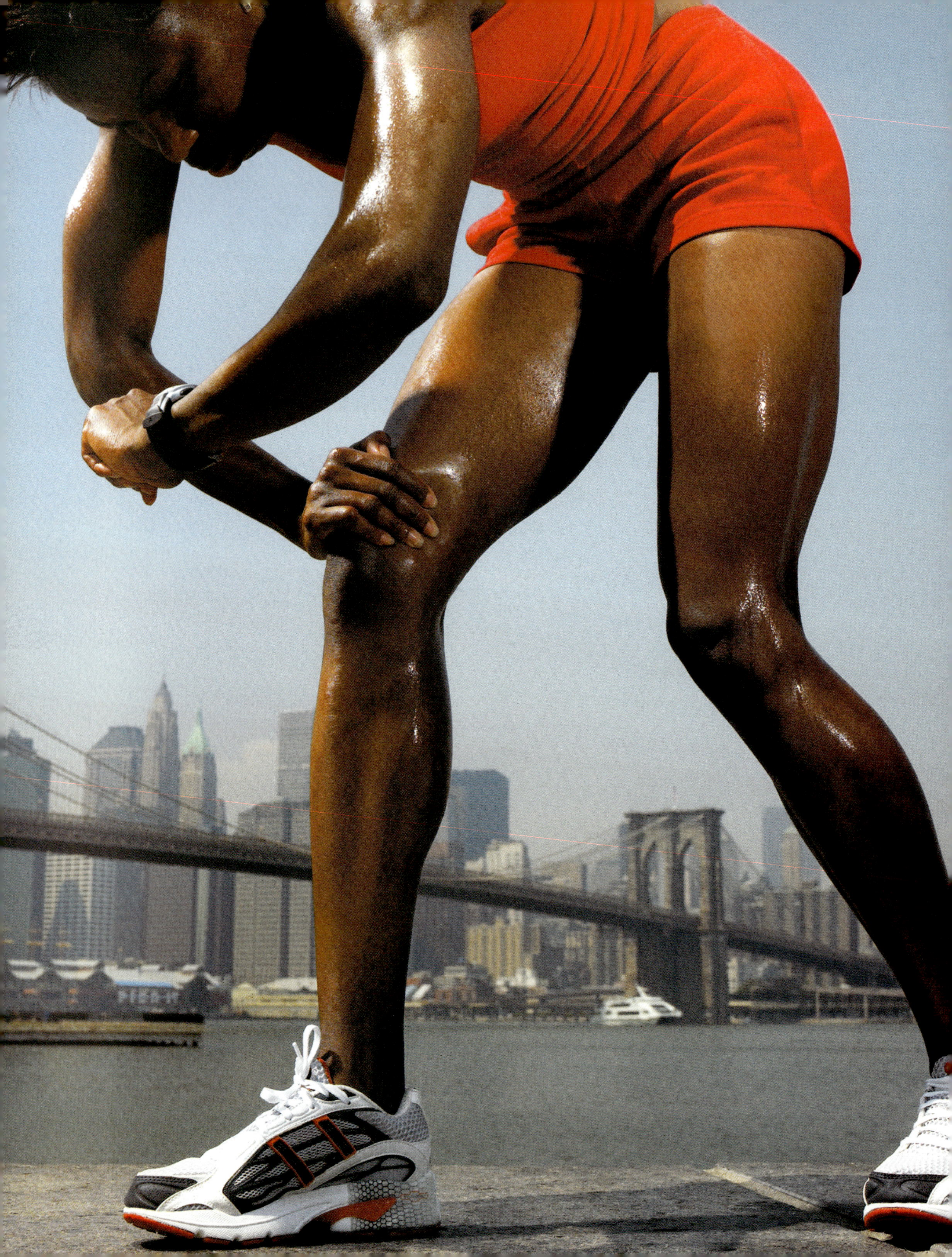

Hydration

Effect of dehydration

The human body is made up of nearly 70% water and dehydrates rapidly during exercise through sweating – to the tune of 1-2 litres per hour. Once you are around 2% dehydrated (1.5kg if you weigh 75kg), your performance could drop by 10% (a staggering 24 minutes if you were aiming for a four-hour marathon).

We all know about the importance of drinking enough water for our health, mental performance and during exercise, but 75% of us in the UK are still walking around chronically dehydrated. When you're training for a marathon, your fluid needs increase and being properly hydrated becomes essential to maximise performance, reduce risk of injury (tight dehydrated muscles tear more easily) and optimise use of glycogen stores.

Most experts have historically recommended drinking about two litres of fluid a day, but this broad-brush approach doesn't suit everyone. If you have a heavy training schedule, run in warm weather conditions or are very light with a low sweat rate, your needs could be very different. A more practical method, and a more recent recommendation, is to look at the colour of your urine (yes, honestly). It needs to be pale and clear, rather like a nice, crisp Sauvignon Blanc – anything darker than that (see chart) means you're already dehydrated and you need to drink more.

Get into the routine of drinking little and often throughout the day, and avoid gulping down pints at a time (your bladder will thank you for it). Keep a glass on your desk, carry a sports bottle with you on your journey to work or when you're out and about, and make sure you drink a bit more in the two hours before and after exercise.

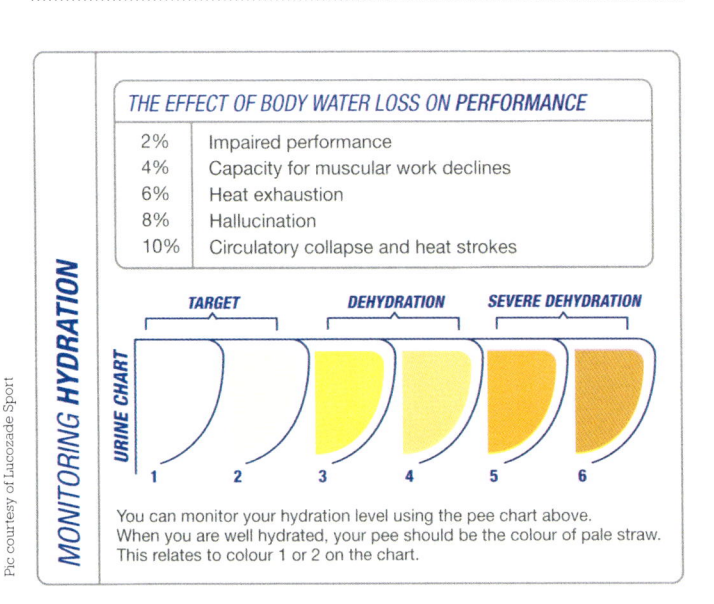

DON'T RELY ON THIRST
By the time your thirst mechanism kicks in, you're likely to be already dehydrated, so drinking needs to become a habit rather than a response.

THE EFFECT OF BODY WATER LOSS ON PERFORMANCE

%	
2%	Impaired performance
4%	Capacity for muscular work declines
6%	Heat exhaustion
8%	Hallucination
10%	Circulatory collapse and heat strokes

MONITORING HYDRATION — URINE CHART

TARGET: 1, 2
DEHYDRATION: 3, 4
SEVERE DEHYDRATION: 5, 6

You can monitor your hydration level using the pee chart above. When you are well hydrated, your pee should be the colour of pale straw. This relates to colour 1 or 2 on the chart.

Pic courtesy of Lucozade Sport

Hyponatraemia

It is possible to drink too much water in a marathon and put your health seriously at risk. This is an extremely rare condition (although becoming more common) known as hyponatraemia, by which the electrolyte levels (sodium and potassium) in the body become dangerously diluted and, in extreme cases, it can cause death. Exercise-induced hyponatraemia is on the increase, with women more at risk for reasons yet not understood by experts. It is also a concern among fun runners, who are out on the course for a longer time and more likely to have a higher sweat rate. Experts recommend that, in a marathon, you should use a sports drink containing electrolytes (often provided on the course) and try alternating sports drinks and water at each aid station.

Dr Nick Gibbins (ultra runner and marathon medic) says that the number of cases of hyponatraemia at long distance races is on the increase. 'This is mainly due to the fact that marathon and ultra-marathon running is enjoying a massive increase in popularity and the group of runners who are most at risk are first-timers and 'fun-runners''. He recommends not being 'over-zealous' in your efforts to rehydrate – so don't guzzle loads of water at each water station and use a drink containing electrolytes during the race. Symptoms include dizziness, vomiting, 'fuzzy head' and swelling of the fingers. If affected, have an electrolyte drink or eat something salty.

The Ultimate Guide to Marathon Running

● NUTRITION

Recovery products

Sometimes your legs might need a helping hand to recover properly. Here are some handy products that might make a difference

Dynamint Muscle Balm £14.49 (237ml)
Any runner entering a clubhouse for the first time will be knocked out by the aroma of different embrocations as athletes douse their legs in an array of different products to beat niggles, pain or just give tired muscles a lift. If you're looking for a natural option, then Dynamint is a great alternative. The main ingredient, peppermint oil, helps increases blood flow to affected areas whilst eucalyptus and tea tree oil provide a gentle cooling sensation followed by a feeling of 'applied heat'. The addition of calendula oil (a skin conditioner) ensures that Dynamint also soothes and moisturises muscles and soft tissue. The product is great for soothing aches and pains and for helping alleviate muscular and joint problems (and it smells a whole lot healthier than other balms too!).
▸ www.wellnessdirect.co.uk

Runner's Remedy £25
Runner's Remedy is a nifty little product from the US that's now available in the UK. The brand's line of cold compression therapy products are uniquely designed by medical professional to help alleviate the most common running related injuries. Targeting shin, Achilles and arch problems, the products combine the benefits of compression and low-profile icing therapy. Essentially, they are a compression bandage with a flexible pocket that enables the runner to insert one of the low-profile ice packs to really target the cold benefit of the ice in the right area. Everyone knows the acronym RICE (Rest, Ice, Compression, Elevation): with Runner's Remedy dealing with ice and compression, the rest (and elevation!) is up to you!
▸ www.runnersremedy.co.uk

Tiger Balm £4.19
Tiger Balm is one of running's little secrets. Once you have used it, you become attuned to its unique smell and can give other fellow runners in the know, the nod. This little pot is one of the world's leading topical analgesics, with a soothing action that relieves muscular aches and pains. Tiger Balm's formulation contains camphor, menthol, cajuput oil and clove oil. And you are spoilt for choice; Tiger Balm comes in two versions, Tiger Balm white, with a higher concentration of mint oil, and Tiger Balm red with its comforting aroma of cinnamon oil.
▸ www.tigerbalm.co.uk

Neo-G VCS Ankle Support £17.50
Neo-G offers a range of breathable supports with embedded silver (to increase blood circulation and accelerate rehabilitation) and aloe vera, to get you through the times when you need that extra help with a niggle or an injury. This range includes an innovative back support featuring an elasticated lacing mechanism, an ankle support, wrist support, a knee support, tennis/golf strap for epicondylitis and a sacroiliac belt to help relieve upper and lower back pain. The whole range is 100 per cent breathable and has Neo-G's exclusive 'targeted compression' system.
▸ www.neo-g.co.uk

The Ultimate Guide to Marathon Running

A quick way to stop feet, knee and back pain naturally

Footdisc insoles £29.95

footdisc 'dynamic' insoles are designed specifically for sport. The key concept is to enhance performance and alleviate 'issues' caused by excessive pronation and fatigue. With more than 70 per cent of runners suffering from injury each year, footdisc works to provide a solution for many sporting injuries, such as plantar fasciitis, shin splints, knee pain, blisters etc.

The key design feature is the Dynamic Arch Cradle (DAC): it guides the foot to a more efficient position throughout the entire gait cycle. Energy - normally dissipated by the cushioning materials in other insoles - is stored. In the propulsion phase, the DAC returns this stored energy, helping to propel you forward during toe off. The insoles come in three different arch heights, accommodating your customers' varying foot types.

With manufacturers increasingly looking at 'lightweighting' their shoes, the manufacturers of footdisc Proactive insoles claim they provide the "perfect interface between the foot and the minimalist shoe to allow the increased proprioception that 'barefoot' running affords".

➤ www.footdisc.co.uk

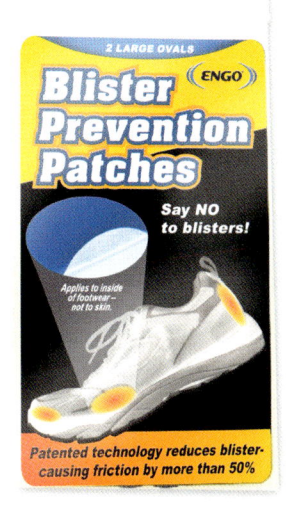

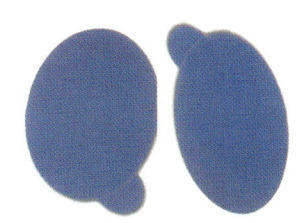

ENGO Blister Prevention Patches £5.99

As the name would suggest, these patches are a different way of tackling the problem of blisters. Rather than wait till you have a blister, you apply these to stop you getting one in the first place. Uniquely, they are applied to the footwear and not to the skin. Blisters are caused by friction which in turn causes heat which results in skin shearing and blisters forming. More than 40 per cent of marathon runners will suffer from this condition. ENGO works by substantially reducing the friction between footwear and your feet so the problem never arises. Each patch lasts for about 300 miles of wear. If you are on a training run and start to feel a hot spot, you can stop and apply a patch secure in the knowledge that you will not develop a blister during the rest of your run.

➤ www.goengo.co.uk

The Strassburg Sock £38

Does that first step in the morning or after getting up from your couch feel like someone stuck a knife in your heel? If this is a description of you, you're not alone. Millions of people each year are faced with this type of pain. While there may be other causes, the most common is plantar fasciitis.

The Strassburg sock is a patented solution for the treatment of plantar fasciitis. Essentially, you wear the Strassburg sock as a 'night splint' - the sock holds the foot in place so that it can't move while stretching the calf, all while you're sleeping!

A study, published in The Journal of Foot & Ankle Surgery, pitted two therapies against each other: the Strassburg Sock and a traditional calf-stretching regimen. Each was used to treat a group of patients suffering from plantar fasciitis. The night splint was found to be far more effective than stretching, helping patients recover in an average of 18.5 days versus 58.6 days for the stretching regimen. Users of the Strassburg sock not only like its effectiveness but also its streamline design over other night splints, which can make it hard to get a good night's sleep.

➤ www.fitbrands.co.uk

Foam roller from £11.50

There's nothing better to roll away your muscle pain than a foam roller, and using one is simple! Working some areas may take a bit of practice and some body contortion. By positioning your body with the area you want to work on top of the foam roller, you can use your weight to massage and release tight knots in the fascia, or connective tissue that surrounds your muscles. Control the pressure by applying more or less body weight on the foam roller and using your hands and feet to offset this as needed. It's helpful to try a variety of positions and see what works best for you. If you find a particularly painful area (trigger point), hold that position until the area softens.

➤ www.physiosupplies.com

The Ultimate Guide to Marathon Running

● NUTRITION

Carb loading

IN THE days leading up to a marathon, most runners will undertake a process known as carb loading. The theory is to get as much glycogen stored in your body as possible by eating more carbohydrate and reducing your training volume (known as tapering – see page 141). This, combined with clever fuelling on the day, will help you last the distance and, hopefully, prevent you hitting the dreaded 'wall'.

Hitting the wall is every marathon runner's biggest fear and happens when your body simply runs out of glycogen stores. You can feel disorientated, dizzy and exhausted, and your pace slows dramatically – and there's nothing you can do about it. All thoughts of target times generally go out of the window and just finishing the race in one piece is all you can think about. Runners often experience it around miles 18 to 22, or after about two-and-a-half to three hours. Starting too fast is often the culprit because you use up precious glycogen stores by running too quickly too soon. Good pacing, carb loading before the race and correct fuelling during the marathon should give you the best chance of avoiding the 'wall'.

HOW TO CARB LOAD

About three to four days before your marathon, start to increase the amount of carbohydrate in your diet, while at the same time reducing your intake of fat and protein. Your calorie requirements will be lower because you won't be training, so focus on increasing the percentage of carbohydrate in your diet. Focus on main meals of rice and pasta, and add lots of carbohydrate-rich snacks and sports drinks. Eating little and often is the key.

Depending on your training volume, your normal training diet should include around 4-5g carbohydrate/kg per day. When carb loading, this needs to go up to about 8g-10g per kg. To put this into practice, consider our example runner Joe Smith. He eats around 375g of carbohydrate per day when in normal training. During the three days prior to his marathon, he needs to ramp this up to about 600g. This requires him to eat an additional 225g of carbohydrate per day for those three days before the race.

You can do this by adding extra pasta to your evening meal, having sports drinks instead of your normal water, snacking on fruit, cereal bars and even sweets during the day, extra toast at breakfast and having a carbohydrate-rich pudding (sponge with fruit and custard for example).

As we've already discussed, your normal training diet should have a carbohydrate percentage of 55-60%, but, for optimal carb loading, you need to get this up to around 75%. Increasing the total volume of food you eat won't achieve that percentage unless you reduce fat and protein levels at the same time. So focus on choosing high-carbohydrate meals and snacks, but low fat and protein. Pasta with carbonara sauce, for example, is rich in carbohydrate, but also has a high fat content because of the bacon, cream and eggs. Opt instead for a seafood tomato sauce, which gives you a better percentage of carbohydrate from the meal.

AND FINALLY...

There is a slight downside to all this carbohydrate loading. Your body will also store extra water (3g for every 1g of carbohydrate) and it's quite common to gain weight during this carb-loading phase – which could be anything up to 1-2kg. Standing on the start line feeling slightly bloated and heavy can feel uncomfortable, but is totally normal and very necessary – it is actually just water and glycogen stores, not body fat. Think of this extra 'weight' as your essential fuel tank, which will power you through the race!

THE HISTORY OF CARB LOADING

Carb loading was invented in the 1960s, when it became apparent that storing extra glycogen in the body before an event helped athletes run for longer. Back then, it was based on an initial 'depletion' phase for three days, which involved heavy training and a low-carb diet to 'strip' the body of glycogen. Then, a few days before the race, athletes would 'flood' their bodies with glycogen – by resting and eating a high-carb diet. The theory was that, being 'stripped' of glycogen, the body would be encouraged to store much more energy than normal. It had many pitfalls, though, and runners found the depletion stage exhausting and counterproductive to race preparation. Since then, further research has proven that the more gradual carb-loading process that we use today is equally beneficial and much less risky.

The Ultimate Guide to Marathon Running

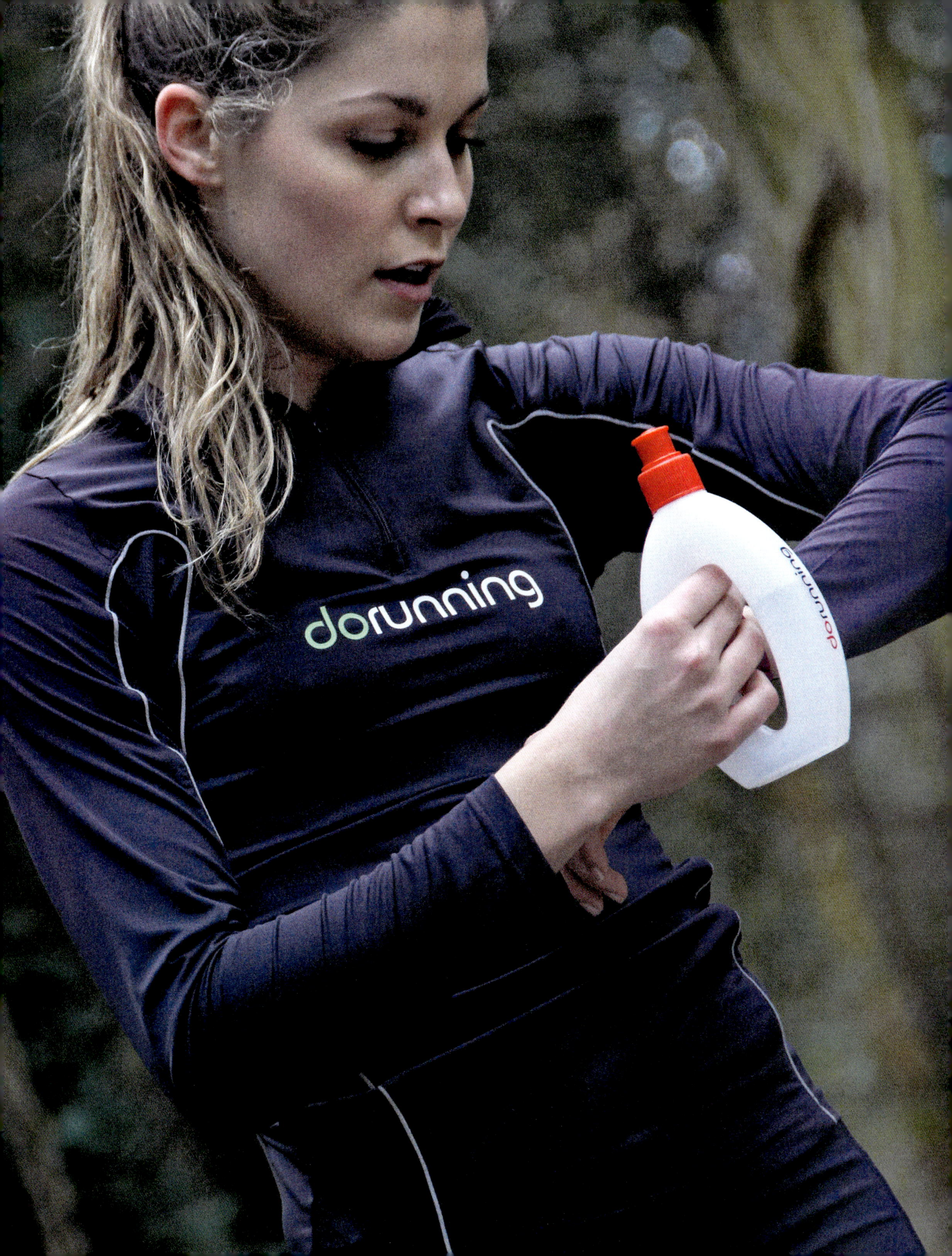
dorunning
dorunning

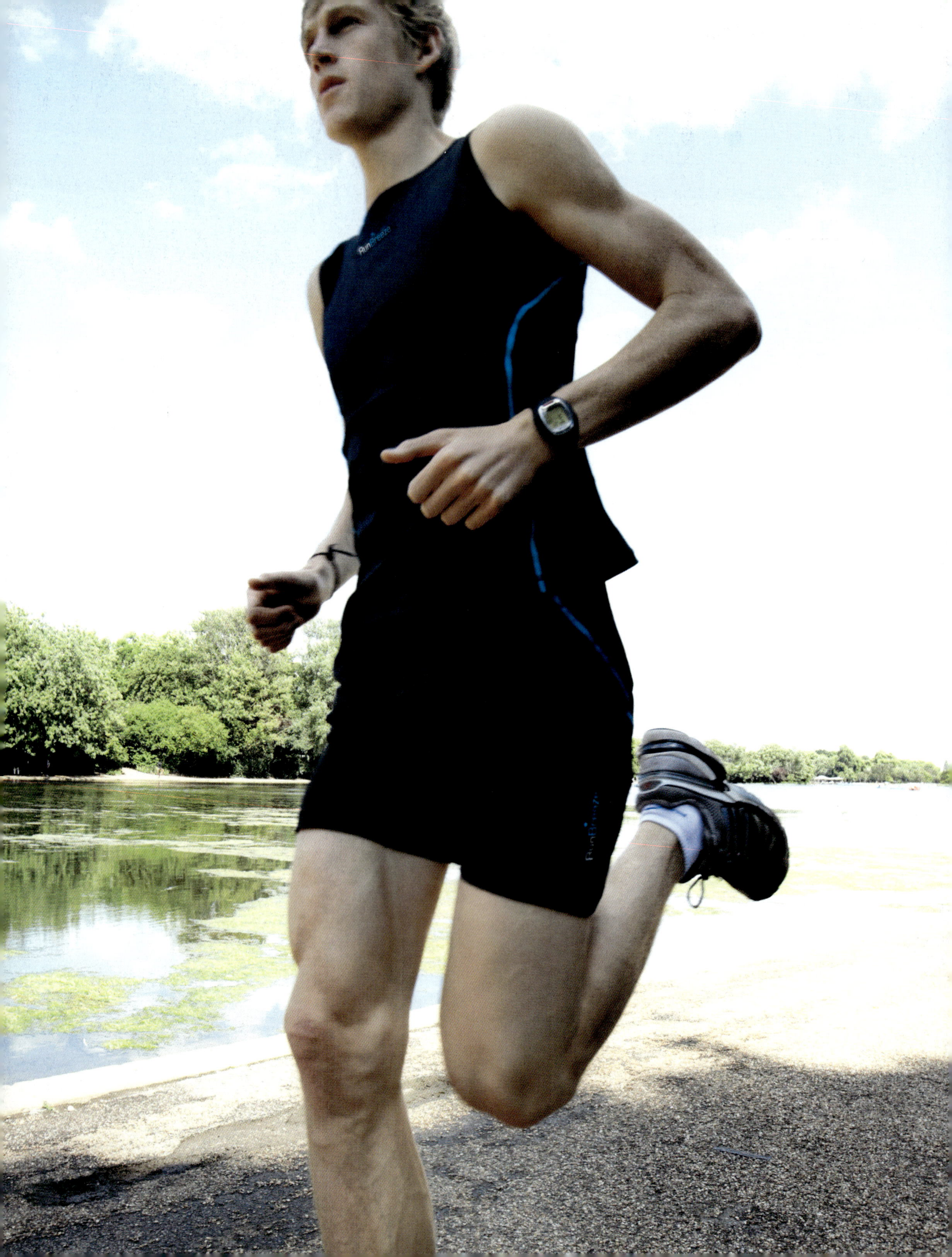

Part six

CHECK THE TECHNIQUE

What is running technique? Why is it so important and can you do anything to improve yours? The annals of history are littered with examples of successful runners whose technique has defied the rule books, but has done little to impede their results. Look at Paula Radcliffe, for example: you'd think that nodding head and awkward arm movement would hold her back, but it's difficult to argue with the most successful female marathon runner of all time. In fact, Paula is a model of efficiency, as are most elite marathon runners. But what lessons can we mere mortals take from the marathon greats to apply to our running? This chapter reveals why technique and running efficiency are so important, why stride length matters, how to breathe and how to hold your arms when running. If you can apply just one of these, you'll see the benefits.

> **YOU'LL FIND THE MORE DIFFICULTIES YOU HAVE ON THE WAY, THE MORE YOU WILL ENJOY YOUR SUCCESS** — JUHA VÄÄTÄINEN, FINNISH DISTANCE RUNNER

The Ultimate Guide to Marathon Running

● **TECHNIQUE**

Fine tuning ● Drills ● Posture ● Stride length ● Heel or toe?

MORE THAN MEETS THE EYE

Running technique. It seems so simple, doesn't it? Just put one foot in front of the other and keep going. Yet there's more to the apparently simple process of our running than meets the eye (or road). Indeed, most novice marathon runners wonder whether they need to change their running technique or style. They worry that if their technique is uneconomical and inefficient, their times will be slower and they might be more susceptible to injuries.

We know, through biomechanics studies, that top-level marathoners have very high levels of running efficiency and economy. In other words, they cover the ground, at a given pace, using less energy and less oxygen than slower runners. Efficient and economical runners maintain their cruising speed for longer using less energy.

It's clearly an advantage, then, to have an efficient, biomechanical style – and it's safe to say that these measures are prime factors in a runner's success.

However, studies have inadvertently revealed something else very interesting. It appears that running biomechanics are highly personal and come from the unique way our body is put together – our skeletal framework, flexibility, muscle size and length, joint tightness, coordination, and even our muscular strength all contribute to our particular (or peculiar) running gait.

Logically, then, even elite runners will have a very wide range of running styles and, if you watch them effortlessly cruising around the running track, you'll notice that they all move differently.

Although there is a theoretically perfect running style, it is highly unlikely that it can be applied to you with any success. But the question remains: can we improve our running technique, even in little ways? Some coaches think that, because we are all so structurally different, we are probably better off not tinkering with our running style. Consciously trying to change the way we run might actually inhibit our performance – some of the odd things about our running technique may actually be compensating for the way our body is designed. These coaches say that it is unwise to force a particular technique change on a runner if it doesn't feel right.

Most coaches know the frustration of 'correcting' a runner's form so it looks pretty good, only to have the runner revert back to his or her old, ungainly style when fatigued from hard training or in the middle of a race.

Changing your running technique is, therefore, a tough proposition because, in many cases, the apparently inefficient movements that you have may actually be counterbalancing a structural deficiency elsewhere in

Choose technique flaws that you think need to improve the most

The Ultimate Guide to Marathon Running

the body. One university study even found that, after working on runners' techniques for five weeks, they did not improve their efficiency or economy.

However, as is typical with research, for every study about changing running technique that finds no improvement, there will be one that finds the opposite. Another university study found that specific gait manipulation produces a marked improvement in running economy in trained female distance runners.

Thus, most coaches conclude that you should not tinker with your running technique unless it is really inefficient, and then only if some of your running quirks actually inhibit your performance.

But there are things you can do to make sure your running technique is not slowing you down. Below are some things you should try to eliminate from your running technique because they misdirect your energy or make you consume more oxygen, both of which will fatigue you earlier.

DON'T...
... have excessive head movement and rolling
... flap your wrists
... have much vertical oscillation (upward movement)
... bring your knees up high in front of you

The Ultimate Guide to Marathon Running

● TECHNIQUE

Drills for Technique Improvement

HERE ARE some tips you can start working on immediately to make your running technique more efficient. These drills can simply be incorporated into your normal training runs. However, trying to make all of these changes at one time will, obviously, be too much – you won't even be able to memorise the list, let alone try all of the changes. Just select two or three related ones before your training runs and think about them through the entire session. Do this for several training runs in a row and, when you think these changes have become permanent, move on to other items.

Alternatively, do a special session on the track, one or two days a week, when you do nothing but concentrate on improving aspects of your technique. Choose technique flaws that you think need improving the most.

These drills are easily done. Choose the changes you want to make and start slowly running around the track while maintaining the new technique change. When you think you've got it, speed up slightly and maintain your new form. Keep speeding up until you are at your cruising race pace and hold that for a lap or three.

When you start your next technique-drill workout, always start by replaying the technique changes you made in the previous session.

Here is a review (right) of good running technique points that you might consider working on if you feel you are deficient in any of these areas.

DO...

...start being aware of your technique and form while running

...have your foot strike the ground under the bent knee after the leg has begun to swing back under the body (not on its way out)

...land on your heels and roll through to the forefoot for take-off. This means you should not be striking the ground on your forefoot or midfoot so your calf muscles absorb the shock

...keep your centre of gravity over your foot

...transfer your weight evenly from one foot to the other

...strive for optimal stride length

...occasional leg turnover workouts to increase stride frequency

...make sure your arms and legs are synchronised in the same rhythm

...try to run with a rhythmic flow

...run with 'light feet' and bounce quickly and lightly off the ground

...monitor your breathing pattern

WATCH YOUR ARMS

Your arms help balance and propel you forward, so their action is very important for you to operate with maximum power. Swinging your arms sideways across the centreline of your chest and allowing your elbows to cross forward past your torso are two things that sabotage your arm action. These, fortunately, are relatively easy to eliminate. The following checklist will help you achieve a great arm action.

ARM ACTION CHECKLIST

- Carry your hands forward near your chest with a short compact arm swing and back as far as the seams of your pants
- Move your arms forward and backwards from the shoulders
- Keep your shoulders down, arms and face relaxed
- Keep your elbows at (about) a 90 degree bend
- Carry your arms between your waistline and chest
- Relax your wrists and hands
- When speeding up, drive more with your arms

Start being aware of your technique and form while running: you'll notice a difference in how you feel

The Ultimate Guide to Marathon Running

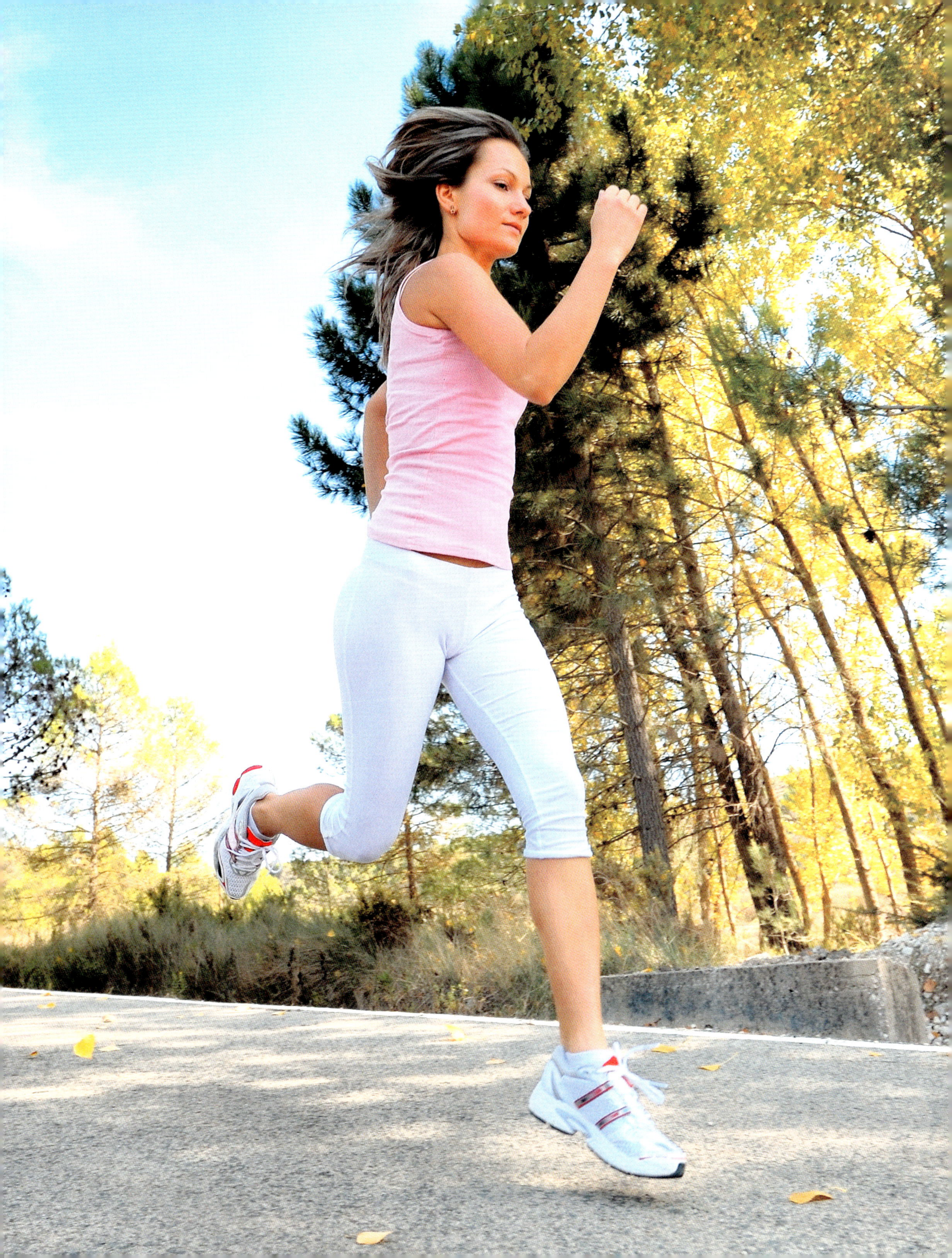

● TECHNIQUE

Your Running Posture

WHY IS good running posture important for marathoners? When we're running in the early stages of a marathon, our core muscles (back, abdominals, trunk) are still fresh, so our posture tends to be upright, which is how we want it. But, as the miles go by and we start feeling fatigued from the lactic acid that builds up in our system - along with other muscle malfunctions - our postural muscles fatigue and we slump forward, like a tired sack of potatoes. The result: shorter stride length and slower leg turnover, resulting in a slower time than you deserve.

By concentrating on strengthening the core muscles, you'll be able to hold your upright posture for longer before the rot sets in. This makes a huge difference to your finishing time (not to mention how you feel during and after the marathon). See a personal trainer at your gym to set you up with a 30-45 minute core muscle workout. The exercises might be on a BOSU Resistance Trainer, a Gymball, or using some weight-training equipment. Ideally, you should do exercises on all three of these.

Doing some resistance training each week also helps in another way. As mentioned above, runners with good mechanical efficiency exert greater force and power for the same amount of energy as runners with poorer efficiency. A few strength-training sessions each week benefits the beginning marathon runner tremendously by improving their leg power, thus increasing the force with which your legs spring off the ground. This translates into less fatigue towards the end of the marathon and a faster time.

Another benefit of strength training is that it reduces injury rates among marathoners. Having stronger arms, legs and trunk muscles means that any weaknesses you might have in your joints will hold together better under the strain of running.

Now that you've strengthened your postural muscles, what should your posture look like when you're running?

Firstly, let's cut out any bad habits we might have in our trunk. The worst culprit is excessive side-to-side torso movement when running - remember, you're trying to move forward, not sideways. By concentrating on driving your arms directly forward you will eliminate this because your body follows your arms when running.

LET'S LOOK AT GOOD POSTURAL PRACTICES TO CONCENTRATE ON WHEN RUNNING - HERE IS AN IDEAL CHECKLIST FOR YOU TO CONSIDER

MAKE SURE YOU...

push your chest up slightly

lean trunk slightly forward, but maintain an upward body position

keep your upper body forward, over your feet

The Ultimate Guide to Marathon Running

Stride Length for Marathoners

TWO WAYS you can increase your speed are by increasing the number of steps per minute (stride frequency or turnover) and increasing the distance of each stride. Research shows that distance runners are better off concentrating on increasing stride length, and sprinters are better off increasing both leg turnover and stride length.

Here's a chart showing what happens when we speed up our running pace.

It shows that the primary way we speed up is by increasing stride length until we get below five-minutes-per-mile pace, something that's not likely to happen to most of us running a marathon!

Running Speed	Stride Frequency	Stride Length
8:03/mile	180/minute	1.1 metres
6:26/mile	180/minute	1.4 metres
4:50/mile	180-200/minute	1.85 metres

As a general rule, then, increasing your stride length will increase your distance-running speed. Only when running at faster speeds, such as the final sprint at the end of a marathon, does stride frequency become a factor. Thus, it's a good idea for you to do the occasional drill aimed at lengthening stride, but still do the occasional fast leg turnover drill to ensure you won't be left behind in the final half mile of your marathon.

How much should we increase our stride length? Every runner has an optimum combination of stride length and stride frequency, depending on their individual mechanics. Your foot should land directly under the knee. Avoid over striding because, when your foot lands too far in front of your body's centre of gravity, it causes a braking motion. Too short a stride and you'll consume too much oxygen because you will not be efficient at that pace either.

The important thing is to establish your best cruising speed and stride length at which you consume the least oxygen. Try running at varying speeds on a flat 400m track: you can find the pace at which you seem to cruise in a comfortable, fast steady state. You should be able to self-select an optimum pace and stride length for yourself.

The Ultimate Guide to Marathon Running

● **TECHNIQUE**

How Marathon Runners Can Increase Stride Frequency

You can experiment with your stride rate by checking it the next time you run, by counting how many footfalls you make in one minute. If your rate is less than 180, you may benefit from increasing the cadence.

STRIDE HEIGHT

Something closely related to stride length is stride height, another great energy waster. Running with exaggerated up and down bouncing vertical movement is very uneconomical for the long-distance runner because your energy is best transferred into horizontal movement instead of upward.

BREATHING RATE AND PATTERN

It is important that you are aware of your breathing pattern while running. It's a useful tool for gauging training and racing pace. Most elite runners breathe with a 2-2 rhythm. That is two steps while breathing in (one with right and one with left foot) and two steps while breathing out. Most good runners take about 180 steps per minute, giving them about 45 breaths per minute.

During particularly hard racing, runners might breathe with a 1-2 rhythm and, running slowly, at a 3-3 rate. Breathing rates can be used to monitor your pace during a race. Running up hills for instance, you can try to maintain a 2-2 rhythm, to ensure you're maintaining a constant intensity and not getting into an anaerobic zone.

As far as breathing in through your nose and out through your mouth, this should happen naturally. However, if you don't seem to use this pattern, you don't need to be concerned as long as you're breathing in enough air to meet your running demands. Most runners breathe in and out through both nose and mouth anyway.

These then, are some tips to help you examine the most important aspects of your running technique and, perhaps, make modifications should you decide it's necessary. Just remember that you are unlearning an old neuromuscular habit that you have developed over many years and, therefore, it's unrealistic to expect immediate changes. It's wiser to gradually make a few changes at a time and then introduce another modification or two once you think your technique adaptations have become permanent.

The Ultimate Guide to Marathon Running

Heel or toe?

Can changing your technique make you run faster?

ANYONE WHO'S seen Britain's marathon world-record holder Paula Radcliffe run will know that her technique is not exactly poetry in motion. With a strange nodding head movement and staccato style, she looks, frankly, ungainly. Yet, she's actually a model of efficiency.

Why? Elite athletes such as Radcliffe and Ethiopian running legend Haile Gebrselassie are both forefoot strikers, which means their toe hits the ground first when they're running. Conventional wisdom - and certainly many of the long-established training principles - have encouraged the polar opposite, suggesting that runners should land heel first and roll through onto the toes (most shoe manufacturers think the same and build their shoes accordingly).

But is one running style really any better than the other? Does it make any difference and, if so, why can't we all be forefoot runners?

Practice makes perfect

At the Hawaii Ironman 2008, Craig Alexander came from behind in the bike section to claim a stunning victory and post the fastest run split of the day (2hrs 45mins). He gave the credit for his success to his Newton Running shoes, a brand, new to the UK, that encourages the runner to run toe-first. Alexander's performance reignited the debate among runners about what is best: forefoot or heel striking.

Most coaches have, until recently, advocated heel striking as the most effective technique. But this way of thinking may have come about simply because most runners they looked at were heel strikers (a quick look at Gebrselassie in full flight would soon convince them otherwise).

In reality, there is no 'right' or 'wrong' way to run: it's about what works for you. Coaches have long since given up trying to convince Paula to change her 'nodding head': you simply can't argue with a woman who's run 2hrs 15mins for a marathon.

Still, it's worth remembering that mankind ran with no shoes at all for thousands of years. Anyone who's interested, should take off their trainers and run barefoot to see what they do naturally. More often than not, people find that they strike the ground with their forefoot - so is this our 'proper' running form?

To check your stride rate, count how many footfalls you make in one minute

NEW TECHNIQUES

By landing on your forefoot, with knees and weight over your centre of gravity and, therefore, absorbing the shock in your muscles and not in your joints, you are potentially avoiding many of the impact injuries that running can bring. But, as well as being useful for injury prevention, purists believe forefoot running is actually faster.

The method has been popularised by Dr Nicholas Romanov. His book, The Pose Method, claims forefoot running is the best approach and gives a detailed description of the technique, while outlining the many drills that can be done to transfer from heel striking to forefoot running. Many individuals (former world triathlon champion Tim Don being one) and running clubs have now adopted the forefoot approach, claiming it is more efficient and faster than heel striking. Danny Dryer, an ultra-distance runner and author of Chi Running, also promotes a forefoot style, this time based on Tai Chi, which he says is 'a more effortless way of running'.

The Ultimate Guide to Marathon Running

● **TECHNIQUE**

How to forefoot run

THE THEORY

LAND: Instead of pounding the ground on your heel, position your foot perpendicular to the ground and land on the centre of the forefoot. Your foot will not settle level to the ground. Don't be afraid to let your heel touch the ground; this is perfectly natural as long as your first impact is not on the heel.

LAND

LEVER: As your mid-foot/ forefoot hits the ground, the Newton shoe absorbs the shock that running creates. The energised lugs in the shoes' forefoot (four extended plastic areas) act as levers, just as your foot does inside the shoe.

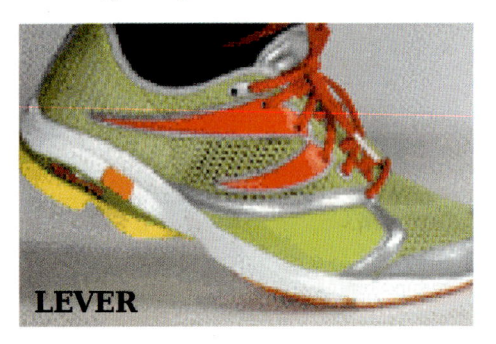

LEVER

LIFT: As you pick up your knee to begin a new stride, the lugs thrust out of the mid-sole with a burst of energy that turns into forward propulsion. With that burst of energy behind each stride, the effort it takes to lift the knee is greatly reduced. This action will power you through your stride with minimal effort.

LIFT

The Ultimate Guide to Marathon Running

Are you running naturally?

TYPE 'BAREFOOT RUNNING' into Google and it will return nearly two million results. That's hardly surprising given the amount of media coverage the trend received in 2010 - and the often-sensationalist headlines that accompanied it ('Barefoot running may be better for you' being just one example).

And while it might still be a niche proposition in the UK, in the US, it's taken off in a big way, with brands setting up to cater specifically for the trend. Of course, the term 'barefoot running' among shoe manufacturers is something of a misnomer: almost all the major brands have something in their portfolio that is classed a 'barefoot' shoe, but these vary dramatically in weight and structure (and the foot is not actually 'bare').

But one thing that all the protagonists agree on is that barefoot or 'natural running' improves proprioception - the ability of being aware of your body, its posture and its movement.

Traditional thinking has put much of the technology into the heel of a running shoe. But having a large lift under your heel makes it very difficult to imitate barefoot running. That's why 'barefoot' shoes are always minimal in their design: there are no built-up heels and any cushioning under the heel is virtually at the same level as that in the forefoot (the percentage drop from rear to forefoot is significantly reduced over a conventional cushioned shoe).

Barefoot or natural running is not for everyone and is something that should be practised steadily over a long period of time: don't simply stick on a pair of barefoot shoes and run an hour. Gradually get used to the sensation of the lower profile footwear and try and run on a flat, off-road surface. It can be a great way to strengthen your feet and reduce injury.

NEWTON SIR ISAAC £99
The Sir Isaac has been designed with a bevelled heel and toe to help guide the runner easily into the mid and forefoot position. The same design has been used with the lugs to make the running motion smoother and give you a stable feel will in the forefoot position.

ON RUNNING CLOUDRUNNER £120
Running exposes our feet to both vertical and horizontal forces. It is the horizontal - or forward-pushing - impact, says On, which can result in increased muscular breakdown and associated injuries. While traditional cushioned running shoes absorb the vertical impact, they fail to effectively reduce the horizontal forces.

On's solution to this is CloudTec cushioning: 13 circular pieces of rubber incorporated into the outsole designed to work effectively together to activate the feet. During the footstrike phase, these 3D elements fold back and cushion the landing by allowing the foot to glide into the ground impact.

SAUCONY PROGRID KINVARA £85
Saucony says the Kinvara is "the epitome of minimalism": the Kinvara's ProGrid LITE unit is only 20% of the thickness of normal ProGrid. But this is definitely a training shoe, rather than a racing shoe, and it has been tested by typical runners over 400 plus miles.

MERRELL BAREFOOT TRAIL GLOVE £82
Merrell's Glove line is designed to "help engage the feet for a more natural stride" by moving the wearer off the heel and "encouraging forward momentum to a mid-foot landing with lower impact and a more aligned and efficient gait". It has a streamlined profile and, featuring a synthetic leather and mesh upper and the Merrell Omni-Fit lacing system and hugs the foot well.

The Ultimate Guide to Marathon Running

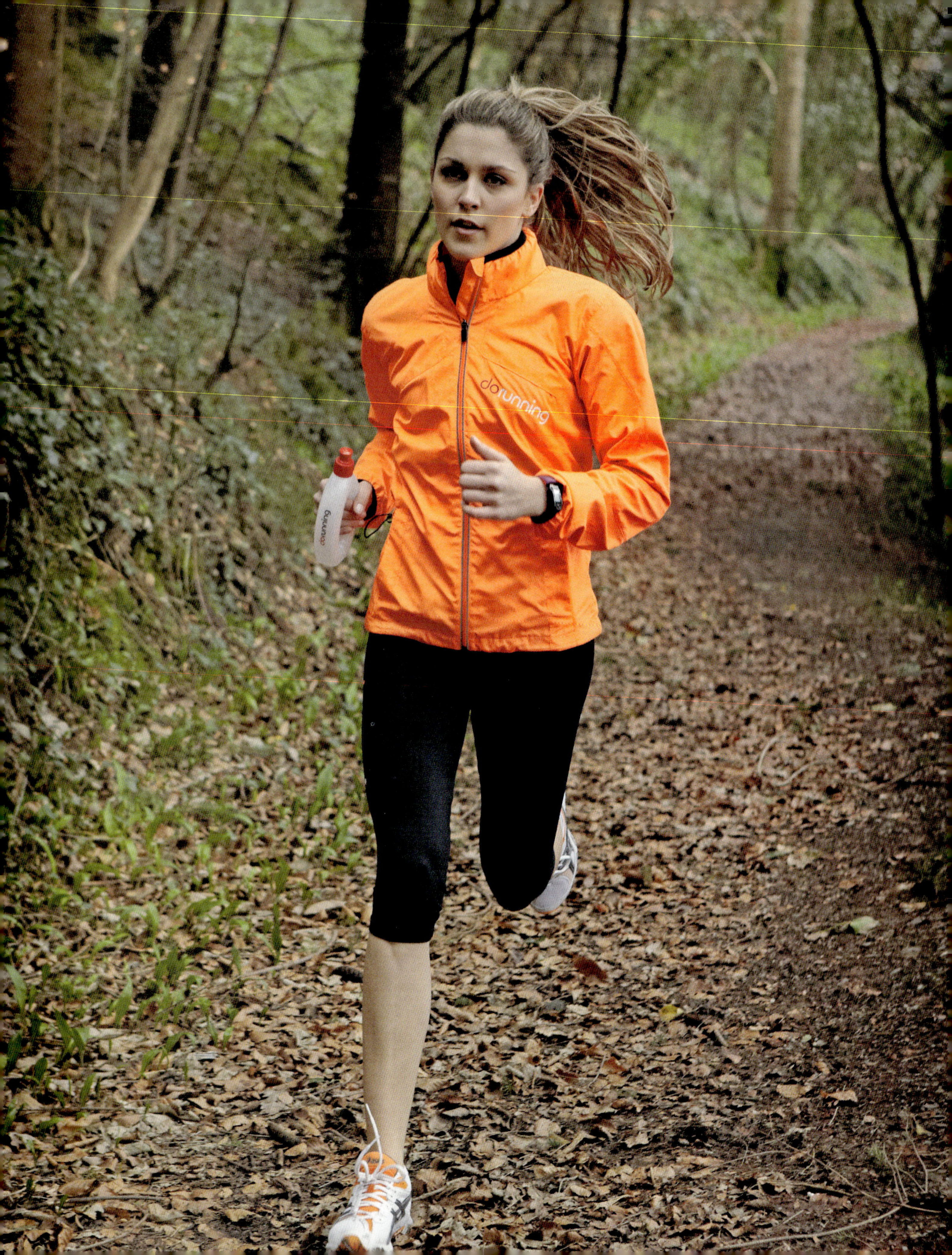
dorunning

Expert's view

Can you reduce injury problems with forefoot running?

CHARTERED PHYSIOTHERAPIST and podiatrist Alex Drummond, of the Drummond Clinic, in Maidenhead, believes forefoot running could have significant benefits with regards to joint impact, tendon/muscle stress and overall session fatigue.

'Forefoot running is an aggressive style of running and those who are unsure should have their running gait assessed to see if forefoot running is for them,' says Alex. 'The technology and concept that has been incorporated into the forefoot [of the Newton] can be likened to the technology used by all of the conventional shoe manufacturers who have designed their own rear-foot cushioning and mid-foot transition plates – but it's in a different place.'

Granted, forefoot running might not be for everyone. But it does present an interesting – and, arguably, less injury inducing – style of running that could see people run further and faster. If that's not incentive enough to try, then what is?

Research shows that distance runners are should concentrate on increasing stride length

The Ultimate Guide to Marathon Running

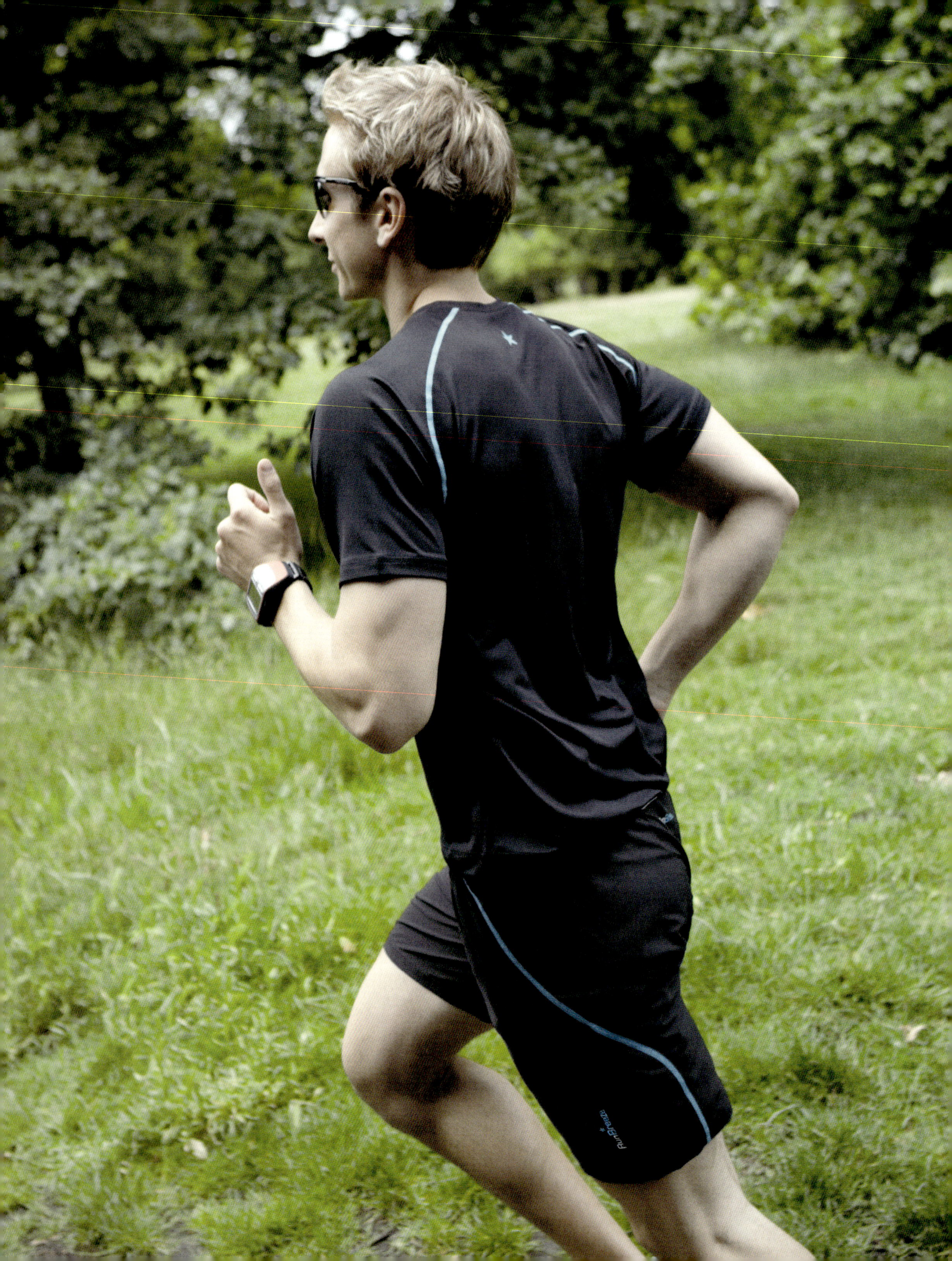

Part seven

TALKING TRAINING

No book on marathon running would be complete without a chapter on what to wear. But this isn't about fashion, it's about finding the shoes and kit that are right for you, and that will make your whole marathon experience one to remember. Pity the runner who wears the wrong shoes over 26.2 miles!

Your shoes and kit are ultimately down to personal preference, but, in this chapter, we lay down some basic rules for choosing the right running shoes and what you'll need to wear if you're preparing to run a marathon, no matter what weather conditions or temperatures you find yourself training in. You'll learn the difference between pronation and supination, the characteristics of various shoe categories and which clothing fabrics work best in what conditions. It's a complete guide to choosing your marathon kit!

YOUR CHOICE OF RUNNING SHOE CAN MAKE THE DIFFERENCE BETWEEN HAVING A GOOD OR BAD EXPERIENCE AND WHETHER OR NOT YOU STAY HEALTHY — OR GET INJURED

The Ultimate Guide to Marathon Running

● TALKING **TRAINING**

Goal setting ● Which schedule ● Diary ● Time management

PUTTING THEORY INTO PRACTICE: THE TRAINING

As you embark on your incredible, life-changing marathon journey, be prepared for one certainty: the road is rarely a smooth ride. Getting to the start of a marathon can be as much of a challenge as getting to the finish line. The path is often littered with frustrating obstacles - injury, illness, family, work deadlines, social commitments, health problems and poor weather - which can put a real dent in your training programme. It's how you deal with these that will be the key to your success.

Most runners, at some point, will have to face and overcome certain challenges - some more than most. But overcome those challenges and, when you cross that finish line, you can be assured of the most amazing sense of achievement - and that's guaranteed. That is what makes the marathon such an incredible, inspiring feat - it's not just the distance of the race, it's the journey to get there that makes it so tough.

Whether you simply 'get round' or set a new personal best time, it'll be up there as one of the greatest achievements of your life.

Of course, if you're going to get round the gruelling 26.2 miles, you have to put in the training. But your mental attitude and approach to training, time management, preparation and, of course, the race itself will also play a huge part in whether or not you make it - and how much you enjoy the journey.

RESPECT THE DISTANCE

Regardless of whether you want to set a personal best or just 'get round' the marathon course, you have to put in the miles. Underestimate the challenge ahead and you'll live to regret it. Having said that, with progressive training and the right preparation, the marathon is surprisingly achieveable for just about anyone. The epic growth in distance running around the world is testament to the increasing popularity of the marathon and just about everyone - from supermodels to celebrity chefs - want to be part of it.

If you're relatively new to running or, perhaps, not as fit as you'd like, we recommend you get a full check up with your GP before you start training or following any of the programmes in this book. Now is also the time to get biomechanically assessed by a physiotherapist or sports therapist, who will look for muscle imbalances or weaknesses that could cause injury as your mileage increases. You may benefit from some specific core stability and stretching to reduce your injury risk before you even embark on your programme.

Then, get kitted out with the right shoes, clothes for all seasons, a diary to record your training, a stopwatch and some running buddies - and you'll be all set.

The Ultimate Guide to Marathon Running

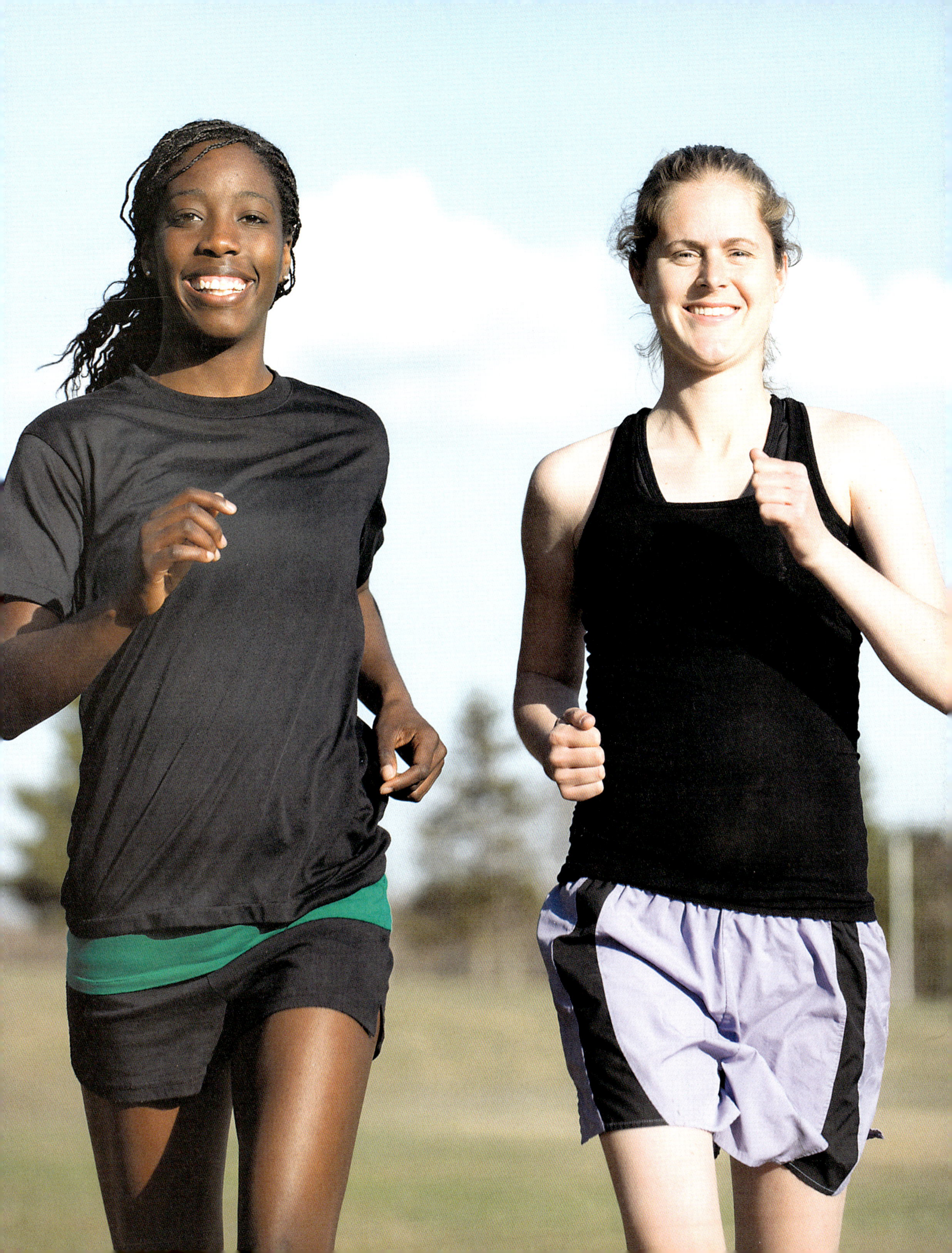

● TALKING **TRAINING**

Set your long-term goal

Before you even begin to start training, you need to set your marathon goal. Why? Because if you don't know where you're going, how will you know how to get there? Set your target, then develop your training plan to reach it.

GOAL SETTING isn't just about a time target for your marathon, aiming for a personal best or knocking minutes off your time. Your goal could be, very simply, just to finish, to enjoy the experience running with a friend, to fulfill a lifetime ambition, to take in the sights - especially in a foreign race - to raise money for a charity close to your heart or to run in memory of a loved one.

Effective goal setting is about taking a long, hard, honest look at why you want to run this marathon and what you want to achieve. If you're a marathon 'virgin' and you don't have a background in running, your goal may well be to just get round and enjoy the experience. Perhaps you do have a time in mind, but is it realistic - and how do you know? Setting goals correctly at the start will help you to plan your training and preparation, and are key to your success and enjoyment.

Your goals may change, especially if you face injury, illness and other problems that disrupt your well-laid plans. You may even find you're fitter than you thought, so end up changing your target to something more ambitious. Be prepared to be flexible and to re-assess your goals as you go along.

A goal properly set is halfway reached
Abraham Lincoln

The Ultimate Guide to Marathon Running

WRITE IT DOWN

A powerful tool when it comes to goal setting is a framework called S.M.A.R.T.E.R. This stands for Specific, Measurable, Achievable, Relevant, Time-frame, Exciting and Recorded. It helps you to set the right goal, which, in turn, helps with your preparation and training; it then helps you know when you've achieved it. You may well have used it before, at work or in your personal life - but give it a try here, when you're thinking about your marathon. Get your notepad and write it all down. Set your main long-term goal, but also short-term targets, then weekly goals and a goal for the race itself. Use the SMARTER framework for all of them.

SPECIFIC
Make your goal clear and specific. Don't just say 'I want to run faster'. How much faster do you want to run? Perhaps your goal is to raise money for charity? But how much, exactly? Set yourself a target. Even if it's your first marathon, you can set a time target, which will not only help with your training, but also with pacing on the day.

MEASUREABLE
How will you know when you have achieved your goal? Having a time target makes it measurable (just ensure it's realistic!), but so does hitting your fundraising target.

ACHIEVEABLE
Is it realistic? You might really want to shave 20 minutes off your marathon time, but, given the new job, the new baby etc, will you really be able to fit in the training to achieve it? Don't set yourself up for failure with an unachieveable target. On the flipside, your goal needs to be challenging to keep you motivated.

RELEVANT
Is this what you want? Is it your goal or is it someone else's?

TIME-FRAME
Give the goal a deadline. This is easy for the race itself, but you might also set interim goals along the way.

EXCITING
Does it rock your world? Is it motivating and inspiring? If not, find a different race or set a tougher target. If it's too ambitious, your goal could feel daunting rather than exciting. For you to get the most out of yourself, it needs to thrill you.

RECORDED
Write your goal down and keep it somewhere you can see it - this helps to motivate you and keep you on track.

The Ultimate Guide to Marathon Running

● TALKING **TRAINING**

Short-term goals

ONCE YOU have your overall goal sorted out, you need to set some short-term targets too. The majority of marathon programmes follow a 12-16 week framework and it can be difficult to stay focused for that length of time. Some shorter-term targets - a couple of half marathons or 10k races - will keep you motivated and give you an idea of how your training is going, allowing you to adjust your programme if necessary.

Breaking this down further, you can also set weekly goals (run 35 miles) and even goals for each session (complete five miles within 40 minutes).

HERE'S AN EXAMPLE (USING THE S.M.A.R.T.E.R. FRAMEWORK):

Steve belongs to a running club and, six months ago, took part in a marathon, which he finished in 4:10 (on an average of 20-miles per week training). He is taking part in the London Marathon in five months and wants to break 4hrs. He has time to train about five hours per week and is prepared, and able, to put in the right amount of training to hit his target. Currently, he runs three times per week. He hasn't done a long run, of more than 10 miles, since his last marathon, so needs to work on his endurance to begin with and increase his mileage gradually. His PBs for other distances are 1:52.35 for a half-marathon and 49:31 for a 10k.

Today's date: 1st November

Long-Term Goal - Sub 4-hours (Specific & Measurable) marathon on 27th April at London Marathon (Time-frame).

This will be an improvement of 10 minutes on my last marathon (Achieveable, yet challenging). Getting a place in the London Marathon with X charity has been a lifelong dream and I also hope to raise £2000 (Relevant & Exciting).

Short-term goals - during the programme (could set exact dates depending on local races)

Sub 1:48 half-marathon

Sub 47:00 10k

Both of these targets are realistic given Steve's fitness, history and overall goal, and they tie in with his predicted time at the London Marathon. If he hits these targets during his programme, he's likely to be on track for his sub 4-hours marathon.

How fast could I run?

There are lots of online calculators that can reasonably predict your target marathon time. Key in a recent race time and it will show you what you could be capable of in the marathon. It is not an exact science, however, and there are many other factors to take into account, which can make the prediction unrealistic, especially if you favour speed over endurance. Another rule of thumb is to take your half-marathon time, double it and add on 10-20 minutes. Try using both methods, which will give you a time band, and then take the average.

The Ultimate Guide to Marathon Running

Which schedule to follow?

Your background in running, current fitness level and long-term marathon goal will be the factors that decide which training schedule you use. We have included three schedules at the back of this book for you to select from.

01
Get Me Round
If you are new to running and your goal is simply to finish the marathon, this is the schedule for you.

02
Marathon Virgin
You may have been running for a while, perhaps even completed a 10km race or half-marathon, but never a full marathon. You're likely to have a target time in mind.

03
PB Hunter
If you've done a marathon before, you'll know what to expect. Follow this programme if you're looking to set a personal best.

● TALKING TRAINING

TOP TIP: 'If you've decided to race a couple of half-marathons, why not use them for different purposes or to achieve different goals? You might choose to run one at marathon race pace or to try out your nutrition strategy. Equally, you might decide that one is a PB race and give yourself a confidence booster before your marathon event.

TAILORING THE SCHEDULES TO YOUR NEEDS

FOLLOWING A schedule helps to structure your training and will provide the correct progression and increase in mileage. But don't follow it blindly: learn to listen to your body and adapt the schedules for your individual needs. If you're feeling tired, take a day off or go for an 'easy' run instead. If you miss some of the schedule because of illness, injury or work pressures, don't panic – don't try to make up for lost time by adding sessions or doing more. Depending on how many weeks you have lost, simply pick up the programme where you should be and carry on. If you've lost more than a few weeks, you'll need to adjust it – especially the overall mileage or long run.

Remember!

The key to getting fitter and faster is in your recovery. Your body adapts and gets stronger when you rest. Always factor in an easy run or day off after a long run or tough session.

The Ultimate Guide to Marathon Running

Other races

All the schedules have one or two warm-up races included in the programme. These serve a number of purposes: 1) to provide a short-term goal 2) to give you an idea of your progress and how well your training is going 3) to provide an opportunity to practise race 'pacing' and 4) they're fun!

10km

A fast 10km can inject a bit of speed into your pace and give you an opportunity for a good blast. Use a 10km race instead of one of your speedwork sessions and try one two weeks before your marathon. This will give you some confidence and make marathon pace feel 'easy'!

Half-Marathon

Aim to complete two half-marathons somewhere in the lead up to your marathon. You'll need about four weeks between them to recover and rebuild for the next one, so check out the race calendar near you, plan them in and enter in advance (half-marathons are very popular and often sell out). Use these events to practise race pacing, nutrition, your pre-race routine (going to the loo, putting your bag in storage) and getting to grips with taking part in a big event. They'll also give you a good target time for the marathon itself.

16 miles and longer

Many marathon runners take part in long races thinking they're doing the right thing. A 20-mile race is completely different to just completing a 20-mile easy run. No matter how hard you try, it's easy to get sucked into racing and end up pushing too hard. It'll take you almost as long to recover from a 20-mile race as it will from the marathon itself and you could end up 'peaking' too early, leading to a disastrous marathon. By all means take part in a race of this length, but race hard at your peril. Treat it as a training run, jog around with a friend and leave your ego at home - make it clear to everyone (and yourself) beforehand and you won't be tempted to go too fast.

The Ultimate Guide to Marathon Running

● TALKING **TRAINING**

Training Diary

Various pre-printed training diaries are available to buy, but you can just as easily use a page-to-view diary or a blank notebook. Keep a track of the following information:

KEEPING A training diary is, without doubt, one of the most powerful and motivating tools you can use. Writing down the training you've done (or not) makes you more accountable - there is nothing worse than seeing a week of blank entries. It will help to keep you motivated and stay focused.

Not only that, keeping a detailed record of distance, times, heart rate, the weather and so on will provide essential feedback when looking back at your training. Seeing your progression and improvement written down in black and white is really motivating and gives you confidence.

> *Date / Time of day (can make a big difference). Weather (was it hot? Raining? Snowing? Slippery underfoot?).*
> *Route / Type of session - steady, easy, intervals, tempo*
> *Distance / Time / Heart rate (resting, average, maximum and recovery - track some or all)*
> *How you felt or other notes (who you ran with)*

DATE - Sunday 15th Dec 8am
WEATHER - Cold and crisp, no wind, frosty underfoot
ROUTE - Snape Wood and Cherry Farm - mainly offroad, fairly hilly
DISTANCE - 12 miles
SESSION TYPE - Steady long run
TIME - 1:42 (2 mins better than last time)
HEARTRATE - Average 145bpm Max 175bpm (on the hills!)

Notes - Felt really good and strong. Ran with Andy and had a good catch up.

DATE - Wednesday 18th Dec 7.30pm
WEATHER - Wet and windy
ROUTE - Club run in town - all pavement, flat
DISTANCE - 6 miles (1 mile warm up, 3 miles tempo pace, 2 miles easy)
SESSION TYPE - Tempo interval
TIME - 52:45
HEARTRATE - Hit 165 average for the 'tempo' interval

Notes - struggled a bit tonight, quite stressed at work, but a good session done and under my belt.

The Ultimate Guide to Marathon Running

Top Time-Management Tips

SIT DOWN ON A SUNDAY NIGHT with your schedule and your diary and plan out your week. Put training sessions in your diary in advance and you'll be more likely to complete them.

GET YOUR LONGEST RUNS AND RACES in the diary at the beginning, arrange to run with friends or take part in group sessions. Everything else will then slot in around them.

IF YOU HAVE FAMILY, get them on side by getting them involved. Children can help make your drinks and be part of your 'support' crew at races. Older children (or your partner) can even ride their bikes alongside you as you run.

RUN WITH A CLUB OR GROUP at least once a week. It provides structure, social interaction and, possibly, coaching if you go to a club - making it more fun and motivating.

GET ORGANISED - none of us have time to waste looking for lost trainers or discovering that your favourite shorts are in the wash. Plan your route in advance, get your kit out the night before, keep your watch, hat, gloves, iPod together in a box near the door.

RUN WITH YOUR DOG. Double up a dog walk and your run and save time. Just make sure you progress your dog slowly if he's not used to running!

STICK YOUR SCHEDULE UP SOMEWHERE you (and the family) can see it. It'll be a constant reminder of your ultimate goal and everyone will know what training you have planned.

The night before a marathon. I always sit down with my training diary and look back at how much running I've done. Seeing it in black and white and realising that I really did do enough training is incredibly motivating and gives me lots of confidence going into the race
        Duncan Collins. PB 2:46.03. 10 times marathon finisher

The Ultimate Guide to Marathon Running

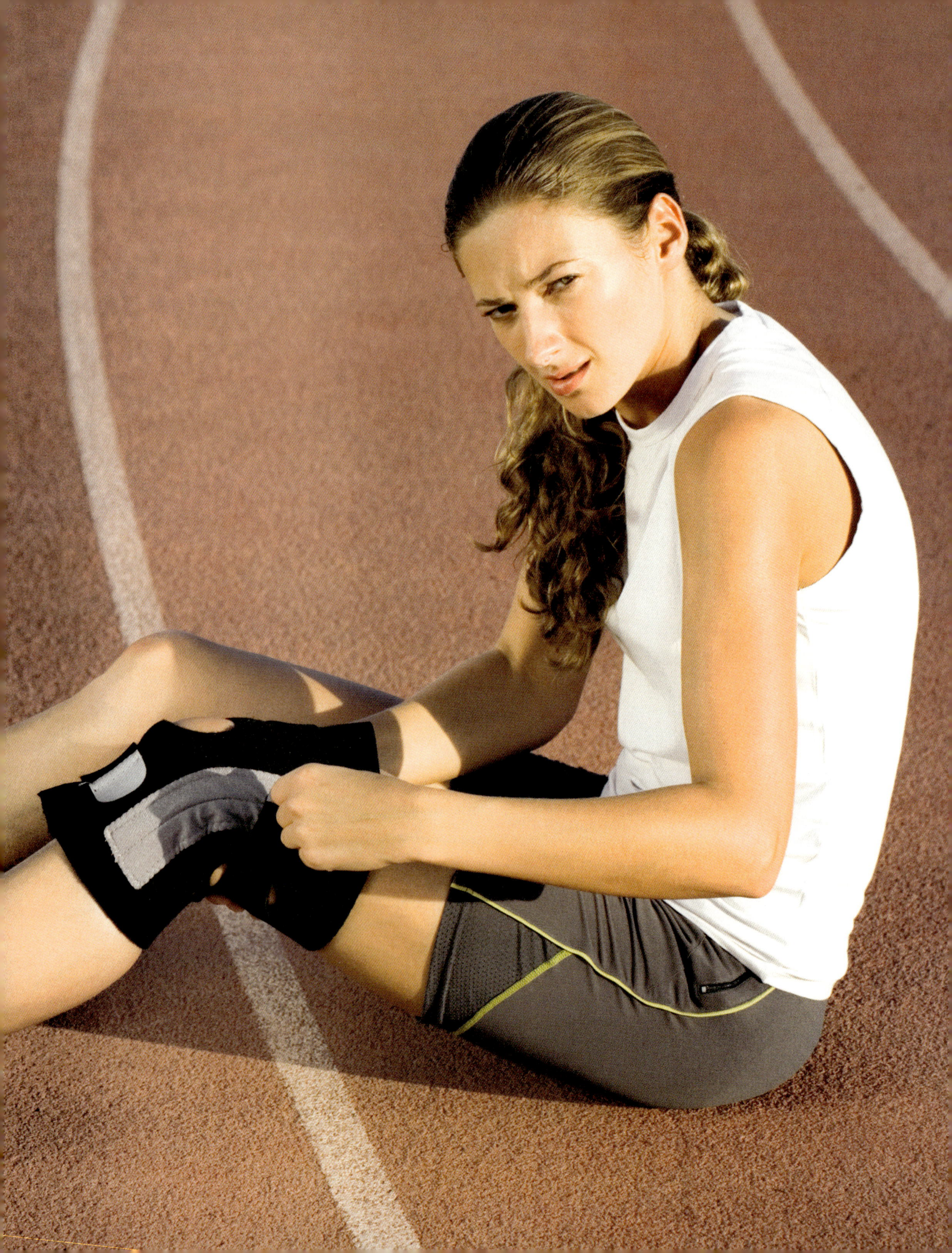

Part eight
INJURY PREVENTION

As someone who's suffered with one injury after another the whole of my running career, the best advice I can give is not to beat yourself up if you can't run. When I was younger, my whole focus was on trying to recover from any number of injuries. Instead of being positive and focusing on other ways in which I could maintain aerobic fitness, I was intent on clearing the offending problem. It's only now, when people more widely understand the benefits of cross training, that I've been able to manage the injury-to-time-running ratio – and put a consistent amount of running together that's enabled me to do a marathon. Even now, I still get it wrong occasionally. This chapter is not an A-Z of types of injury, but rather a guide on how to recognise your injury, deal with it pro-actively and still build your fitness. It is an essential read for anyone who is in the midst of their marathon training.

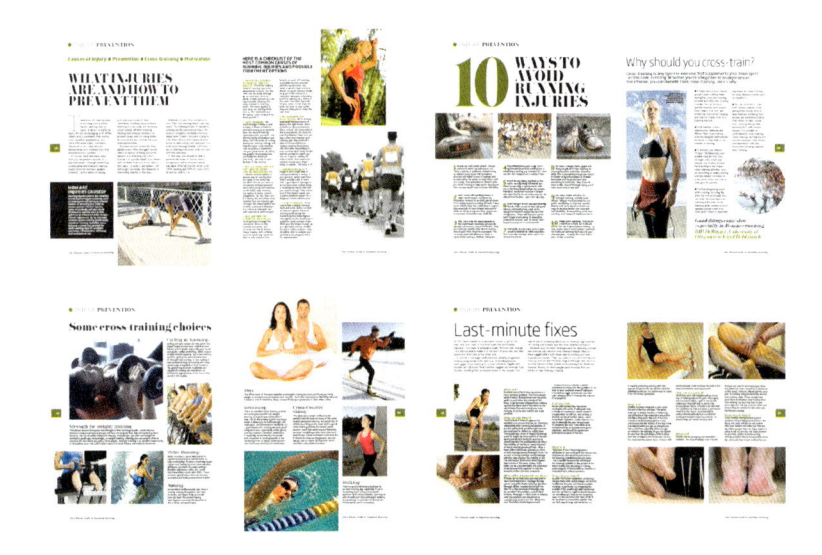

> **YOU HAVE TO FORGET YOUR LAST MARATHON BEFORE YOU TRY ANOTHER. YOUR MIND CAN'T KNOW WHAT'S COMING**
> **FRANK SHORTER**

The Ultimate Guide to Marathon Running

● INJURY PREVENTION

Causes of injury ● Prevention ● Cross-training ● Motivation

WHAT INJURIES ARE AND HOW TO PREVENT THEM

There is an oft-used phrase in running: you're either injured, getting over an injury or about to suffer an injury. It's not encouraging, is it? While there's every possibility that, during your marathon preparation, you will suffer some injury 'downtime', the secret is not to become too disheartened and, instead, turn that downtime into a positive.

Of course, there are many ways that you can prevent injuries, in a physical sense – through stretching, conditioning and strength training (much of which we have already covered) – and in terms of taking practical steps to avoid them. Ultimately, avoiding injury is about listening to your body and knowing when to back off from training, making sure you pay attention to problem areas and not being afraid to incorporate rest periods into your training schedule.

Runners are not known for their patience and often disregard sound advice in favour of doing one extra session or a final long run. Don't. Contrary to popular belief, your fitness will not drain from you if you take a few days – or even a few weeks – off (although, obviously, this depends on the timing relative to the race).

Whether it's your first marathon or your 50th, the training doesn't get any easier. The building blocks of marathon running revolve around putting in the miles to complete the distance in your target time. There's not point trying to cram them all in a short space of time: better to take a long-term approach and build your training steadily, with step ups in training once your body can cope with the demands.

In this way, you should be able to prevent the onset of chronic injury and get yourself to the start line in one piece. After all, it is far better to be 100% healthy and 80% fit than 100% fit and not able to run.

HOW ARE INJURIES CAUSED?

Running injuries come in two varieties. 'Acute' injuries happen suddenly, such as tearing your calf during an interval session or spraining your ankle on uneven ground. 'Chronic' injuries come on gradually and are a result of misuse or overuse, such as shin splints or an inflamed Achilles tendon. Chronic injuries are, by far, the most common type in running (particularly marathon running) and often occur because a runner has ignored the early warning signs of a problem (soreness, inflammation, stiffness) and continued to run.

The Ultimate Guide to Marathon Running

HERE IS A CHECKLIST OF THE MOST COMMON CAUSES OF RUNNING INJURIES AND POSSIBLE TREATMENT OPTIONS

✔ **INCREASING RUNNING MILEAGE OR TIME TOO QUICKLY:** This is the leading cause of running injuries in recreational runners. Use the 10% rule (increase mileage by no more than 10% per week) to help prevent overuse injuries while allowing the body to adapt to training levels. The same applies to your long run: don't go from 2hrs to 2hrs 30mins in one fell swoop - your body will not thank you for it.

✔ **OVER-TRAINING:** Too much mileage is likely to lead to injury in those not able to tolerate running at an extreme level. You need to find the right balance for yourself - and don't be led by what others are doing. Don't be afraid of cutting down your running mileage and injecting some cross-training, such as cycling or swimming, into your programme. By doing less weight-bearing exercise, you'll take the stress off your body - and stay fit (and healthy) in the process.

✔ **NOT ALLOWING ENOUGH REST AND RECOVERY TIME BETWEEN RUNS:** It's a common misconception of people new to running that you need to run every day: you don't. Nor do you need to completely exhaust yourself every time you go out training: comfortable, easy running has a place in every runner's programme. So, too, does rest. It is during the rest phase after exercise that our muscles get stronger. Not allowing this rest leads to continual breakdown. It is critical to alternate rest with exercise to perform well.

✔ **NOT VARYING THE SURFACES YOU RUN ON:** Hard surfaces increase the amount of stress on the muscles and joints, and increase the risk of chronic tissue trauma. Soft surfaces (such as sand) may cause the heel to sink and your foot to slide on push-off, leading to Achilles tendon overuse (Achilles tendonitis). You need to get the right balance: there's no point running totally on grass in the run up to a marathon because, ultimately, you'll be running 26.2 miles on the road. That said, if you do all your miles on the road, the wear and tear on your joints may not allow you to make the start line!

✔ **NOT WEARING THE RIGHT SHOES:** We've already examined the importance of buying the right shoes: when it comes to injury prevention, this is critical. Too many miles in the wrong shoes can cause no end of problems. Make sure you buy a shoe that matches your running gait. Manufacturers also recommend that you replace running shoes every 350-550 miles depending on your running style, body weight and the surface on which you run. So, if you're running 50 miles a week, that means you need to change your shoes every 10 weeks - not long, is it?

✔ **IGNORING NIGGLES:** A niggle is your body's way of saying something is wrong. If you ignore it, what could have been cured by a day or two's rest, a good sports massage or an ice-pack could end up being a troublesome injury that sets you back far longer. Take action and, if that doesn't work, see a sports medicine expert for a diagnosis and treatment plan.

✔ **POOR TECHNIQUE:** Every runner has a unique running style and some styles can lead to overuse injuries. Because running tends to use the hamstrings to a large degree, strengthening the quadriceps is useful for most runners. If you think your technique is poor, go to a specialist running retailer for gait or video analysis - they should be able to analyse your technique and suggest areas for improvement.

The Ultimate Guide to Marathon Running

● INJURY PREVENTION

Most common injuries

Whether it's through overuse, over-training or bad luck, here are the five injuries every runner knows

THE BIG 5

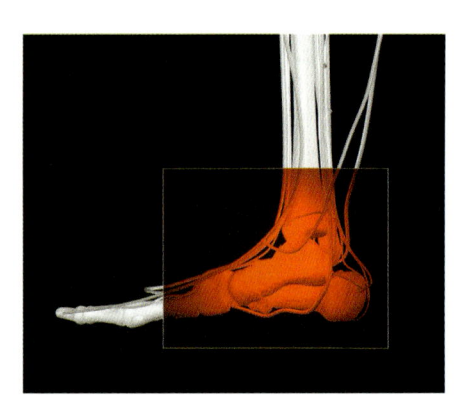

Tendon injury

What is it?
A tendon is a structure that attaches muscle to bone. Tendons consist of parallel collagen fibres that are bunched together. Tendons have poor blood supply. Tendons are designed to undergo a great deal of stress without rupturing. However, it is possible to partially or fully rupture a tendon.

How is it caused?
A tendon that commonly causes problems for runners is the Achilles tendon, which joins the calf muscles to the heel bone. Should the load on the tendon exceed the strength of the tendon, the tendon will begin to break down and the collagen fibres will no longer run parallel. This condition is known as tendinosis. It is painful and, often, the tendon feels thickened and is tender to touch. About one fifth of cases of tendinosis also have a small rupture of the tendon. There are a number of factors that can increase a runner's likelihood to get Achilles tendinosis. These include an increase in activity, changing footwear or the surface on which you run, poor footwear, calf weakness and decreased joint range of motion. If the tendinosis is located in the middle portion of the Achilles tendon, there are specific exercises that can be done to strengthen the tendon, promote re-alignment of the collagen fibres and allow a gradual return to running.

How can it be treated?
A tendon rupture is less common and usually occurs with little warning. This may be managed conservatively or surgically and usually requires a longer rehabilitation period.

Muscle strain or tear

What is it?
Muscle strains are classified according to severity. A grade 1 strain involves a small amount of fibres and there is no loss in strength. Grade 2 strains are more painful because a significant number of fibres are torn. When contracting a muscle with a grade 2 strain, there will be pain. Grade 3 strains are the most severe and involve a complete rupture. These often require surgical management.

How is it caused?
Muscles consist of, what are known as, 'contractile fibres', which produce force and, therefore, motion. Muscles are extremely adaptable and change their fibre type and composition depending on the demands placed upon them. Muscle strains occur when the demands placed upon the muscle exceed the force they can produce and fibres fail. Muscles commonly injured by runners include the gastrocnemius (one of the calf muscles), hamstrings and quadriceps. These muscles all cross two joints and are, therefore, more likely to be injured.

How can it be treated?
If you suspect you have a muscle strain, initially follow the RICE (see opposite) protocol. You will then need to see your physiotherapist for treatment to promote healing and exercises to strengthen the muscle and prevent re-injury in the future. Factors that may lead to a higher risk of muscle strain include poor warm up, muscle overuse or fatigue, poor technique, muscle imbalance, previous injury and poor joint range of motion.

WHAT IS RICE?

- **REST** - put no stress or weight on the injured area for 48 hours. Immobilise if possible.

- **ICE** - apply to the injured area for eight minutes every three hours for the first 48 hours. This reduces blood flow to the injured part.

- **COMPRESSION** - strap up the injured area using a compression or gauze bandage, again, to reduce blood flow.

- **ELEVATION** - raise the injured area to enable blood to flow away from the affected site.

The Ultimate Guide to Marathon Running

Stress fracture

What is it?
The term stress fracture describes a micro-fracture in the bone as a result of repetitive overloading of either the muscle pulling across the bone or direct force through a focal point of the bone. In runners, common stress fracture sites are fibula, tibia (bones of the lower limb) and metatarsals (long bones in the foot). The most common symptoms of stress fractures is pain on loading the structure (weight bearing/running/hopping), but also at rest (e.g. aching at night). On palpation of the affected bone, there is often exquisite tenderness. A stress fracture may not show up on X-ray, so a bone scan may be necessary to diagnose the injury.

How is it caused?
There are a multitude of factors that contribute to a stress fracture. Poor biomechanics, muscle imbalances or weaknesses, low bone density and a lack of flexibility are all thought to contribute to stress fractures. Females are often more prone because they are more likely to have low bone density. There are also a number of training errors that can contribute to stress fractures. A sudden increase in training load, excessive training volume or intensity, inappropriate footwear and inadequate nutrition all lead to an increased likelihood of a stress fracture. A good rule for increasing training volume is 'the 10% rule', by which your volume of training should not increase by more than 10% on the previous week.

How can it be treated?
Treatment for stress fractures involves off loading the affected area with relative rest. This may involve stopping or modifying training in the most mild cases, or immobilisation in the case of larger fractures. Stress fractures take approximately six weeks to heal, at which point there should be a gradual return to running to allow the bone to cope with and adapt to the increased load.

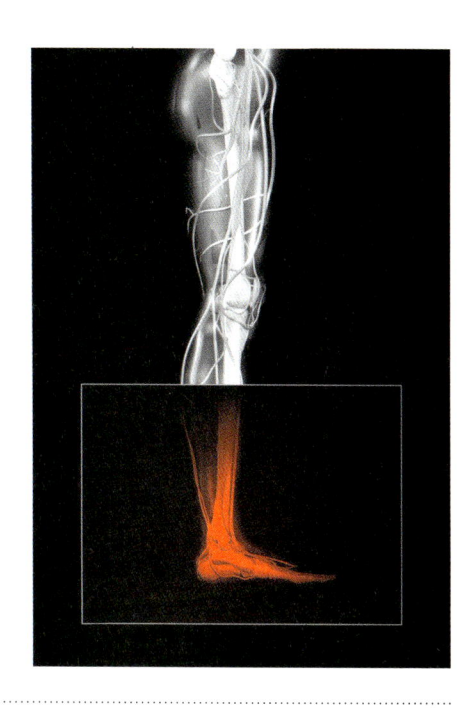

Runner's knee

What is it?
Runner's knee, or iliotibial band (ITB) friction syndrome, is an inflammatory condition on the outside of the knee, brought about by friction between the ITB as it passes over the lateral femoral epicondyle. Pain usually comes on slowly during a run and at the same point with each run. Downhill running often makes the condition worse. Pain normally settles at rest. The main factors thought to contribute to ITBFS is poor pelvic stability and weak hip abductors (gluteals), which increase stress on the lateral thigh.

How can it be treated?
Treatment for runner's knee involves avoiding activity that provokes the pain, soft tissue releases of the ITB and surrounding structures, strengthening the hip musculature, and stretching the ITB and surrounding lateral structures. In more severe cases, a corticosteroid injection may be necessary to reduce the pain. Biomechanical abnormalities need to be addressed to ensure the problem does not recur.

Shin splints

What is it?
'Shin splints' is a broad term for pain along the border of the tibia in the lower leg. There are actually a number of different conditions encompassed by the term 'shin splints'. The most common is medial tibial traction periostitis. This is an inflammatory condition brought on by the muscles of the lower leg pulling on the bone, resulting in traction of the outer layer of the bone. The condition is characterised by tenderness along the lower third of the shin bone. This pain usually decreases upon warming up, but may return after exercise. The morning after a training session, the athlete often reports the pain to be worse. In more severe cases, the pain may remain throughout the run and, if this occurs, must be further investigated to rule out stress fractures.

How is it caused?
There are a number of factors thought to contribute towards medial tibial traction periostitis. Excessive pronation (foot rolling inwards) increases the traction on the bone and, therefore, may be a risk factor. Footwear, muscle length, surface type and fatigue may all lead to increased pronation. Some studies have also shown decreased bone density to lead to an increased risk of this condition.

How can it be treated?
Treatment, initially, is based on relief of pain and symptoms, and you will need to consult a physiotherapist to address any issues that may be causing the injury. Ice, rest and anti-inflammatory medication may all help relieve pain. Massage and trigger-points techniques can be used to release tight muscles. While resting, you can continue to maintain your cardiovascular fitness with cross-training. Non-impact activities, such as swimming and cycling, are good activities for this. If excessive pronation is thought to be contributing to the symptoms, foot taping and, in the longer term, orthotics may help eliminate symptoms.

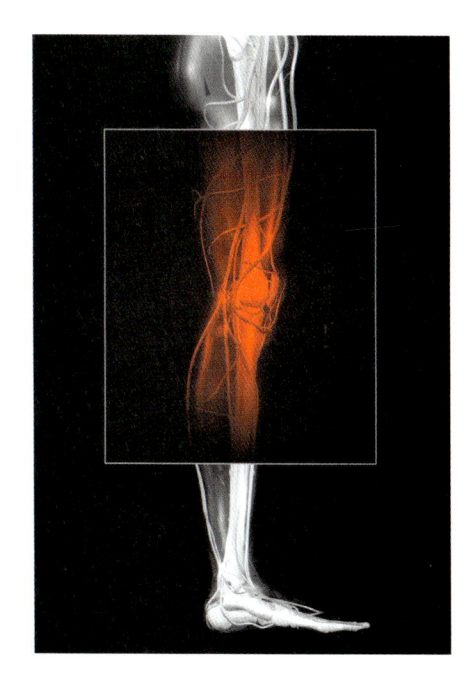

The Ultimate Guide to Marathon Running

● INJURY **PREVENTION**

10 WAYS TO AVOID RUNNING INJURIES

1 Warm up and warm down. Always perform a warm-up before you run. There is plenty of evidence that warming up reduces your injury risk by making muscles less liable to tear or rupture and by lubricating the joints so they're less stiff and creaky. And remember to stretch after you finish running to help return muscles to their resting length and maintain flexibility.

2 Don't wear old running shoes. It might sound simple, but avoid the temptation to revert to an older pair of shoes if it's raining or you're running off-road. These shoes will not have the cushioning or support they once had. It's best to have two pairs of shoes on the go at any one time, so you can rotate them and extend their shelf-life.

3 The 10% rule for most people is the maximum increase per week, not the minimum. Every third week, drop your mileage significantly before moving ahead again from the previous week. The recovery week will allow your body to repair while having a 'relative' rest week.

4 Pay attention to your body. Don't ignore what your body is telling you. If something is hurting, pay attention to it, find out why and change what is making it hurt.

5 Don't do anything too fast or too soon - or anything different too close to race day. A sports doctor told me, in the three weeks before the London Marathon, he sees an increase in people who have tried to do one extra long run. His advice? Don't bother - save it for race day.

6 Don't forget to eat enough healthy foods. Make certain to have adequate calcium and healthy fats (such as the omega fats found in certain fish and fish oil capsules) - these will help your joints. Don't forget to eat plenty of vegetables and protein sources. And, of course, don't forget to eat plenty of carbohydrate!

7 Schedule in rest days, just as you would schedule in other sessions. Don't just take rest days when you're too exhausted to train.

8 Do take a longer-term approach. Many people don't start training for a spring marathon until after Christmas. While this is enough time to get you round, it's better to lay a foundation in October, November and December and have something to build from. Also, if you do have to take time off through injury, you'll have more miles in the tank.

9 Do cross-train. Whether it's strength training, to build more robust, fatigue-resistant muscles and joints; swimming, to maintain aerobic fitness with zero impact or Pilates or yoga to develop better core strength and flexibility, do something other than running. Your body will thank you for it!

10 Enjoy your running. Training for a marathon is hard, but it should still be fun. Mix it up, vary your training, try new routes: savour every session and enjoy the feeling of working hard towards your ultimate goal - crossing the finish line in your chosen marathon.

The Ultimate Guide to Marathon Running

Why should you cross-train?

Cross-training is any sport or exercise that supplements your main sport - in this case, running. Whether you're a beginner or an experienced marathoner, you can benefit from cross-training. Here's why:

Sports such as triathlon are great for maintaining aerobic fitness in periods of injury

- It helps balance your muscle groups. Cross-training helps strengthen your non-running muscles and rests your running muscles. You can focus on specific muscles, such as your inner thighs, that don't get worked as much while running and may be weaker than your running muscles.

- You'll maintain or even improve your cardiovascular fitness. Many cross-training activities are great cardiovascular workouts, so they build on the benefits of running.

- It reduces your chance of injury. By balancing your weaker muscles with your stronger ones, you'll help reduce your chance of injury. Participating in low-impact cross-training activities, such as swimming or water running, will also lessen the stress on your joints, which are often a sore spot for runners.

- You'll avoid getting bored with running. Running day after day will eventually burn out even the most hard-core running enthusiast. Cross-training gives runners a much-needed mental break from their sport, which is especially important for those training for long-distance events, such as marathons.

- You can continue to train with certain injuries, while giving them proper time to heal. Runners suffering from injuries are sometimes told by their doctor to take a break from running during their recovery. But, with certain injuries, it is possible to continue with cross-training. Cross-training can help injured runners maintain their fitness and deal better with the frustration of being sidelined from running.

Good things come slow — especially in distance running
Bill Dellinger, University of Oregon track and field coach

● INJURY **PREVENTION**

Some cross-training choices

Strength (or weight) training:
This allows runners to improve the strength in their running muscles, create balance between unbalanced muscle groups and focus on keeping their legs strong during injury recovery. You can do either resistance training, whereby you use your own weight for resistance (push-ups, for example), or weight training, whereby you use weights (free or machine) for resistance (leg press, for example). Strength training is an excellent opportunity to strengthen your core, which helps runners to avoid fatigue and maintain their form.

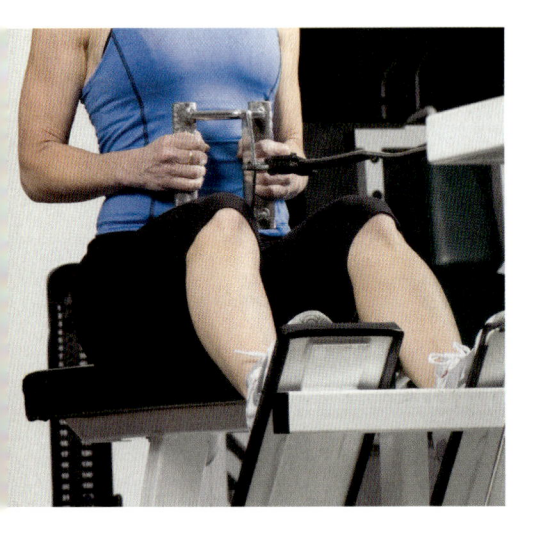

Cycling or Spinning:
Cycling and spin classes are also great, low-impact ways to boost your cardiovascular fitness and strength, especially your quads and glutes. Unlike swimming, which is good to build aerobic capacity, but is non-running specific, cycling has some transference of strength into running. In fact, cycling is very complementary to running and many runners use it regularly in their routines. The world's top Ironman triathletes are capable of running fast marathons on limited mileage because of the hours they spend in the saddle.

Water Running:
Water running is a great alternative for injured runners or as a substitute for an easy running day. It's also a smart way to get in your runs during hot and humid weather. While you can run in the water without flotation aids (vests, belts, etc), you'll find the workout easier with them. There are even special shoes that can increase resistance and make your workout harder!

Rowing:
An excellent cardiovascular, low-impact activity, rowing strengthens the hips, buttocks, and upper body. Just make sure you learn the proper rowing technique to maximise the benefits of this activity and avoid injury.

The Ultimate Guide to Marathon Running

Yoga:
This offers some of the same benefits as strength training because you'll use your body weight as resistance to strengthen your muscles. You'll also improve your flexibility because it involves a lot of stretching. Many runners find yoga a great way to relax after a long.

Swimming:
This is an excellent cross-training activity for running because it's not weight-bearing, so it gives your joints (which take a lot of stress when you're running) a break. It allows you to build strength and endurance, and also improve flexibility. It's a great balance for running because you'll really work your upper body, while giving your leg muscles a breather. Swimming is especially recommended for people who are prone to running injuries or are recovering from an injury. Some runners also find it very relaxing and meditative.

Cross-Country Skiing:
This gives you a great cardiovascular workout and focuses on many of the same muscle groups as running. But you'll skip all of that pounding on the road, so it's a great cross-training activity for runners with injuries. You'll also work on your flexibility because the gliding motion stretches your hamstrings, calves and lower-back muscles. If there's no snow on the ground, you can always use an indoor ski machine, which provides a very similar workout.

Walking:
This is a good activity to substitute for an easy running day, especially if you're recovering from a long run or speed workout. With certain injuries, you may be able to walk pain-free and speed-walking is a good way to maintain cardiovascular fitness while you're recovering.

The Ultimate Guide to Marathon Running

● INJURY PREVENTION

Staying motivated

INJURIES ARE part and parcel of running – it's how you deal with them that makes the difference. No one likes to be injured, but that doesn't mean, just because you can't run, the world is going to end – and with it your marathon plans. Far from it. In fact, you can use the period away from running to improve your general wellbeing.

I don't doubt that, for me, three weeks off with a knee injury in February actually helped me get to the start line of my marathon race this year. For the first couple of days, I thought my race was effectively over: everyone around me seemed to be doing more and more miles, and I was on the sidelines, unable to run. But running is all about adjusting your goals and understanding why I was injured. Like so many before me, I'd simply overdone it, ramping my training up to five or six times a week and upping the intensity: my body simply couldn't cope. The period away from running enabled me to take stock of where I was with my running – and put a training programme in place that would help me get to the start line in one piece. And, of course, I was still able to cross-train. I wasn't able to do anything running specific, but I could still maintain core fitness.

Runners should recognise that, sooner or later, they are likely to develop a running injury. Minor or major, with the training required to run a marathon, it's unlikely you'll run the whole way through. To be sure you can maintain a healthy, positive attitude when you do get hurt, it's always worth incorporating some form of cross-training into your programme on a regular basis, then, if you have to stop running, you'll have other activities you enjoy to keep you fit.

Nobody enjoys sports injuries. The physical damage is bad enough, but injuries cause psychological pain, too. Research shows that injured athletes become depressed and angry, while their energy level decreases. The longer the lay-off, the more depressed they are likely to become. Look beyond the injury – and turn a negative into a positive.

If you learn from your injury, and this helps prevent a similar injury in the future, then you have benefited from the experience
Pete Pfitzinger, coach and former US Olympic runner

The Ultimate Guide to Marathon Running

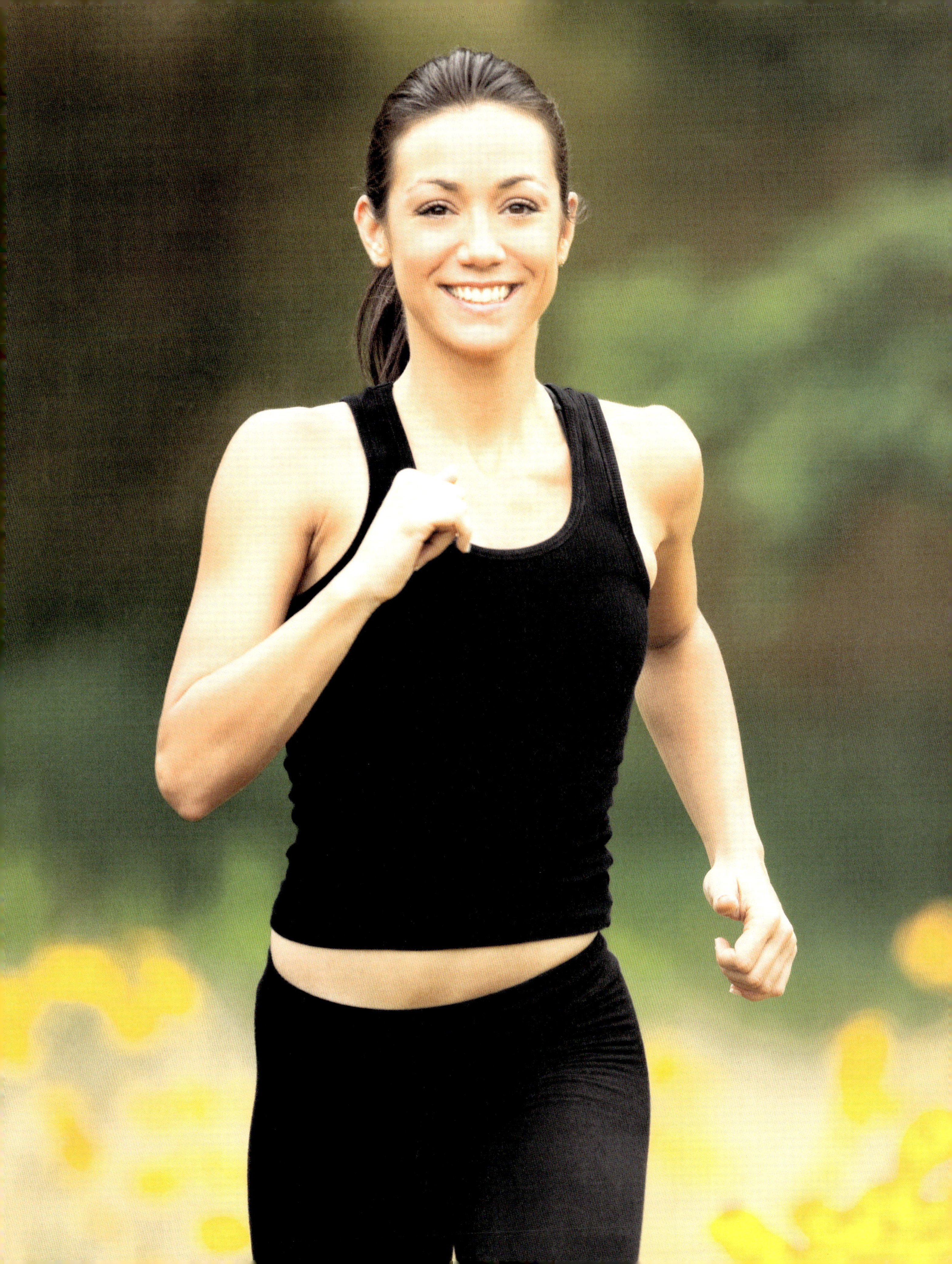

• INJURY PREVENTION

Last-minute fixes

SO YOU have trained for weeks and months to get to the start-line, and, then, in the final week the unthinkable happens - you begin to experience pain. All is not lost, though - it is still possible to make it to the start of your race, and then across the finish line at the other end.

Of course, a thorough, well-planned, suitably progressed training programme is the best way of avoiding injuries and niggles when training for a race. However, niggles and injuries can still occur. Most common niggles are 'overuse' type injuries, resulting from excessive stress to the tissues. This may be due to increasing distances, excessively high volumes of running over a week, and less than ideal biomechanics.

However, poor recovery strategies and not allowing yourself rest time can also result in over-stressed tissues. Many of these niggles affect both those new to running and more experienced runners. They can strike at any point during your training, and not just the latter stages, although they tend to be more common when people are increasing their distances towards the end, or when people panic because they are behind in their training schedule.

RUNNER'S KNEE

What is it?
Iliotibial band (ITB) friction syndrome is a fairly common problem. The ITB is a broad band of fascia that extends from the pelvic girdle to just below the outside of the knee. It can become inflamed from rubbing against the lower end of the femur as you repetitively flex and extend your knee running. It can be very painful and make you limp.

How can you help it?
The first line of defence against this problem is to ensure that you are stretching adequately after running and exercise. If you are particularly prone to tight muscles you may need to stretch on a daily basis. The quadriceps (front of thigh) hamstrings (back of thigh) hip flexors (front of the hip/groin) and gluteal (buttock) muscles all attach into the ITB, and therefore all affect the mobility of the fascia. Stretching each of these muscle groups will help. Using a foam roller (solid foam cylinder) as a form of self-massage along the length of the ITB, as well as the quadriceps and hamstrings, will also help improve the mobility of the ITB and reduce the friction effect against the outside of the knee. Using a foam roller can be uncomfortable and some level of perseverance is required to reap the benefits of this self-help treatment.

What other treatments are there?
If these do not help then you may need to seek some assistance. Massage therapy can be very effective in reducing tightness through all the muscles that attach into the ITB. A few sessions of massage may be needed if the problem is particularly irritable. Massage is a 'kick-start' to helping with the problem and should not be considered a replacement for doing your own flexibility/stretching exercises.

Acupuncture can also be a useful treatment technique for this problem. It can help to relax localised areas of tightness in muscles (trigger points) and can have pain-relieving effects through the release of endorphins.

If all else fails…
For an unfortunate few, the above strategies will not be of adequate help. In these circumstances, when someone is super-keen to still run, and as long as there is no risk of further injury, a local anaesthetic injection can be used on race day to alleviate the pain long enough to complete the race. This needs to be administered by an experienced sports physician, and should be agreed and planned in advance of the race.

PATELLOFEMORAL JOINT PAIN

What is it?
Tightness of the ITB and tightness, weakness or over activity of the connecting muscles can also result in pain around the kneecap (patellofemoral joint pain). This is usually because the tracking of the kneecap (patella) in the groove of the femur is affected, resulting in it being pulled slightly to the outside as the knee is extended from a flexed position.

How can you help it?
As with ITB friction syndrome, stretching, using a foam roller and massage can all help to alleviate the pain and improve patella tracking. In particular try loosening the outside of the quadriceps and hamstrings and the hip flexors. Again a physiotherapist can also show you how to use strapping tape. For this condition the tape tends to be used over or around the patella. This can feel very strange and restrictive so

The Ultimate Guide to Marathon Running

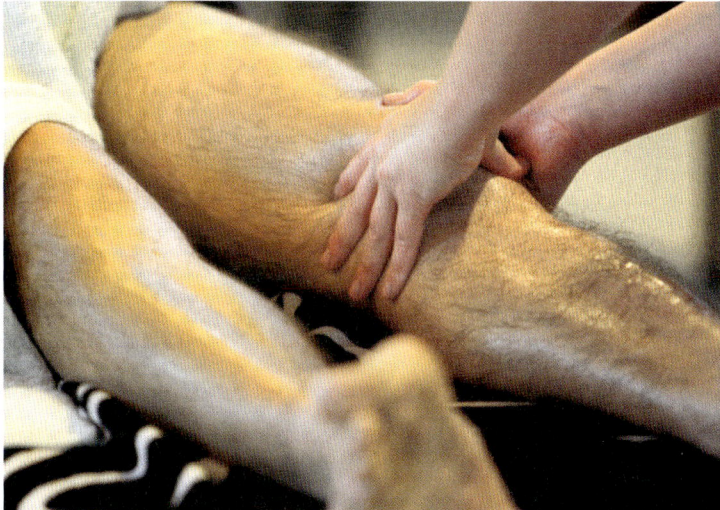

it is worth practising running with the tape on. Acupuncture can also be used for patellofemoral pain in a similar way to using it for ITB friction syndrome.

PLANTAR FASCIITIS
What is it?
Another common complaint is pain under the arch of the foot and heel. This tends to be due to plantar fasciitis, a thickening and stiffening of the connective tissue that acts like a sling under the arch of the foot. It tends to be particularly painful at the attachment into the bottom of the heel bone (calcaneum) when you get up and put your foot to the floor, especially when you get out of bed in the morning. As you put weight on your foot, the arch drops a little to allow your foot to adapt to the surface you are on; this stretches the plantar fascia. If this is stiff and thickened, it will increase the pull on the bony attachment, causing you pain.

How can you help it?
Stretching your calf muscles will go a long way to helping reduce the pain. Massaging the fascia and rolling a golf or tennis ball under your foot will help to stretch the actual plantar fascia. Orthotics can also help this condition as they will place a continuous stretch on the fascia. It is advisable to seek professional help from a podiatrist or physiotherapist regarding orthotics to ensure they are correct for your feet.

UNTIMELY BLISTERS
What is it?
Blisters are an annoying and avoidable problem. You should always race in socks that you are used to wearing so you know they don't rub. If you are prone to blisters in certain areas, then you should pad the area prior to running using products like second skin or blister pads. These usually have some form of adhesive cover to stop them from moving, but you may need to put some tape over the top to secure them and ensure they do not start to slip when your feet become sweaty.

How can you help it?
Using Vaseline over particular areas of pressure will also help prevent blisters. Wet shoes and socks will tend to rub, so look after your trainers and make sure they are dry before you put them on. If you know it is going to rain on race day, use some Vaseline on your feet, and try to avoid running through puddles! Also ensure you have some dry socks and shoes to put on after the race.

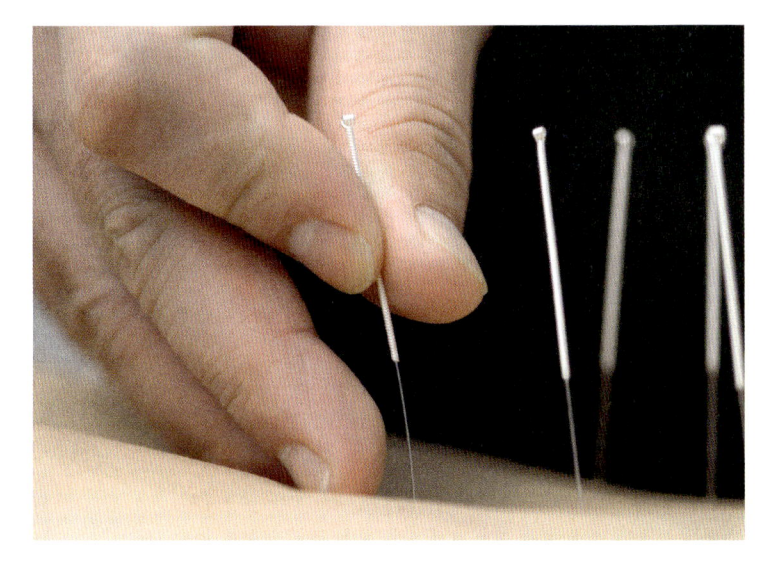

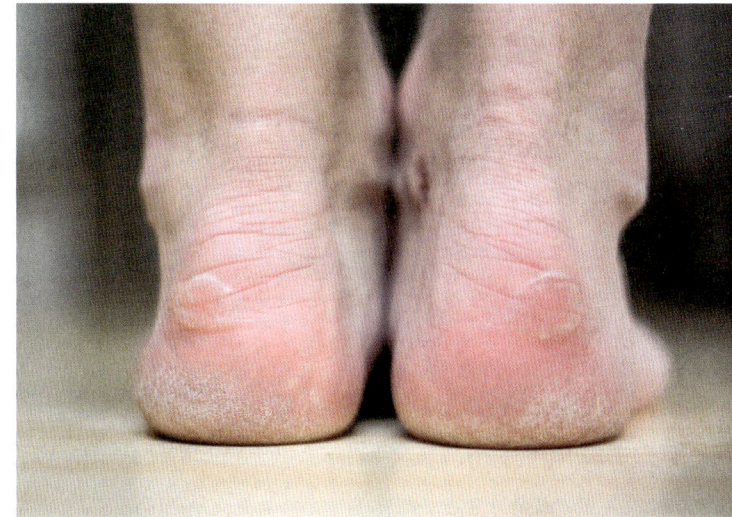

The Ultimate Guide to Marathon Running

Keep running! STEVO

Raise more for charity with Virgin money giving

RACE DAY IS HERE

This is what all the hard work has been for: race day. This chapter helps you put the finishing touches to your marathon preparation and provides practical advice on what to do, and not do, on race day. But don't think we're leaving you at the finish line: we also suggest ways to improve recovery – and what to do next!

The Scout's motto is 'Be Prepared' - and, when it comes to marathon race day, it's a pretty handy phrase for runners to remember.

Given that you've been 'preparing' for this day for several months, making sure you've got your race nutrition ready, your kit sorted, planned your journey, know your start and have a race plan will all help to ease you through what is undoubtedly going to be a difficult - but rewarding and unforgettable - experience.

In reality, your thoughts will turn to race day well before the day itself. You'll probably be plagued with doubts: can I last the distance? What if it's hot? Will I have the right shoes/kit/nutrition? What if I hit the wall? If any - or all - of these thoughts play on your mind, don't worry, it's perfectly normal. Everyone, even experienced marathon runners, will have some nagging doubts, but, provided you have put in the training necessary for your particular goal - and you're not carrying a race-threatening injury - you'll be OK. Take it from someone who experienced all of these doubts, and more, and still made it to the finish line, seven minutes under goal time. If I can do it, so can you.

> **I HAD AS MANY DOUBTS AS ANYONE ELSE. STANDING ON THE STARTING LINE. WE'RE ALL COWARDS** — ALBERTO SALAZAR. THREE-TIME WINNER OF THE NYC MARATHON

The Ultimate Guide to Marathon Running

● RACE DAY

Shoe choice ● Off-road ● Kit ● Compression ● Peripherals

THE WEEK BEFORE

In the final few days before the big race, you'll have a number of things to consider. Given that you'll be on your marathon taper (see overleaf), you should have plenty of time to sort these things out. If it's the London Marathon you're doing, you need to work out when you'll be registering. For London, you can register on any of the four days prior to the Sunday race, although you'll have to take a trip to the Expo at London's Excel Centre to collect your race pack. Some people like to register early; others will register late on Saturday afternoon. It's all down to personal preference, although, of course, if you're travelling down on Saturday, you don't have much choice.

If it's a smaller marathon, or perhaps you're flying overseas to race, chances are you can register the day before. It's also worth finalising your kit choice: you could pick up something at the race's expo, but it's not advisable. You'll want to have experimented with your race-day kit - and shoes - to make sure that what you're wearing is comfortable and right for you. It's also worth considering your nutrition and hydration in the days leading up the race.

Try to drink at least two litres of clear fluid every day in the week before the race. Although this is something that should be good practice, sometimes we just forget. But make a concerted effort, particularly if you know you're going to be running somewhere hot. If your body is hydrated before you race, there's less chance of becoming dehydrated during it.

Top 5 tips

1 Try to get as much sleep as possible in the week leading up to the race. Unless you're superhuman, it's unlikely you'll sleep like a baby the night before. Topping up the sleep-tank in the days before means you'll be able to cope with a restless night.

2 Start to visualise the race. Work out your race plan and know your splits. If it's a 4-hour marathon you're after, try to pick up a marathon pace band at the Expo. It's a good idea to know how fast you need to run - and when.

3 Be properly hydrated for your race. Carry a bottle with you every day in the run up to the race and try to sip a little and often. You could also try limiting your caffeine intake and try to eat sensibly: plenty of carbohydrate in the form of pasta - and try to cut down on processed foods.

4 Pack your race bag early. Make sure you've got all your energy bars or gels, your number, safety pins, vest and anything else you'll need on race day. Make sure you check it the night before - and have a list on which you can tick off the items.

5 Work out your logistics. If it's London you're racing, know which train you need to get and what stop you need to get off at to find your appropriate start. For any other marathon, check the transport situation come race day - some races will run special trains. And check your start time: don't be late!

DON'T
- do a hard session in your final week
- leave everything to the last minute
- experiment with new food in the final few days
- expend too much energy with pointless walking
- worry: you're prepared. Enjoy the down time!

The Ultimate Guide to Marathon Running

THE DAY BEFORE

WITH ALL the hard work done, the day before should be a day of rest, although you'll want to keep your mind active so you don't spend all day thinking about the race. What you do during the day before your marathon can make or break your race, so here are some hints to make sure you get it right

■ **Go for a short run if you need it.** This is as much mental as it is physical, but many people like to know that, after a week of relative inactivity, their legs are still working.

■ **Plan to get up early.** Set your alarm clock and double check it. Give yourself plenty of time to get ready, eat breakfast and get to the race start. If you're staying in a hotel, request a wake-up call, just to be safe.

■ **Try to stay relaxed.** Think positively about all the work you've put into your training. Don't worry if you've had to have time off in the run-up to the race: better to stand on the start line 100% healthy and 75% fit than the other way around.

■ **Eat a carbohydrate-based meal,** but don't experiment with any new food stuffs. Your stomach won't thank you for it on race day!

■ **Get your clothing and gear ready**

Essential items include:
- Race timing chip
- Race number and safety pins
- Running outfit, hat, shoes and socks
- A product to prevent chafing
- Wristwatch
- Your race nutrition

The Ultimate Guide to Marathon Running

RACE DAY

The Taper

THE WORD 'rest' is alien to most marathon runners, especially those who thrive on training hard and pushing themselves. But, if you want to prepare well for your marathon, tapering and a certain amount of 'resting' is exactly what you must do during the two weeks leading up to the big day. Be warned though, many runners find the 'taper' frustrating and, for some, it can be one of the hardest aspects of marathon training. Tapering basically involves reducing your mileage and allowing your body to recover, repair and get ready for the 26.2 mile challenge ahead.

Over the two-week period before the race, you need to gradually reduce the volume of your training, so, come race day, you feel fully rested and raring to go. Some runners describe it as feeling like a 'coiled spring' – which is exactly what you're aiming for.

All that hard training you've done will now be in the 'bank' and you won't lose any fitness by backing off for a few days - in fact, by resting, you'll become stronger. The key to successful preparation is to reduce the overall volume of your training, but keep ticking over with some 'quality' sessions.

Not for everyone, but some runners swear by racing a 10k the weekend before a marathon. If you're a PB hunter with some running experience, and you know you can recover quickly, this could be a great strategy to inject some last-minute pace.

SO HOW DO YOU DO IT?

Scale back too much during the taper and you'll feel sluggish and unfit; but, if you don't rest enough, you could risk feeling tired and lacking in energy for the race itself. A good taper means getting the balance right between training and backing off, so when you stand on the start line you'll feel prepared, rested and confident - just like that 'coiled spring'.

Your taper will depend on your level of training, your goals and your history of running. Low-mileage runners need less taper time than high-mileage runners or those who have done a lot of races or race-pace training. A PB hunter who has been clocking up the miles will need a longer taper – perhaps two to three weeks – than a get-me-round marathon first timer, who can just scale back a bit for 10 days beforehand.

If you feel especially tired coming into the 'taper' period – perhaps because of work or family stress, as well as training – you may need a bit more rest and recovery time. If your training hasn't exactly gone to plan and you've done less mileage than you'd hoped, a shorter taper will probably be fine.

THE PERFECT TAPER

3 weeks before - In an ideal world, your longest run should be two or three weekends before your marathon. No more than 20 miles.

2 weeks before - one last long run, of, say, 15 miles.

Then start to reduce your overall mileage.

Days 14-10 - Reduce overall mileage by 10-20% (perhaps knock one mile off each run or drop one run altogether).

Day 7 - One final 'longish' run of about 10-13 miles.

Days 7-4 - Reduce mileage again by another 10%, but keep ticking over with short runs and a sharp pace.

Follow your schedule, which will have specific sessions depending on your goal.

Days 2 and 1 - Rest or a short, easy run.

The Ultimate Guide to Marathon Running

Final Diet Tips

> I find it really difficult to eat solid food such as a sports bar or a banana when I'm running. Gels are fine, but can make me feel nauseous after a while. Jelly babies are perfect, the night before, I count out 13 and put them in a bag to carry with me. After I hit halfway, I have one at every mile marker — it helps the miles fly by as well!
> Paul Evans - Marathon PB 3:37

7 days before - as your mileage starts to drop, your calorie requirement also drops. Carry on eating as you were at the peak of your training - even just for a week - and you'll gain fat. Focus on consuming quality food over the next week, but start to slightly reduce the overall quantity. If you drop one mile from your run, shave 100kcal from that day's intake.

4 days before - eating small meals often is better than three large meals a day. Keep your blood-sugar levels steady with healthy carbohydrate snacks and regularly spaced meals. Start to carb load (see page 94). Do this by reducing the amount of protein (meat, fish, eggs, beans, nuts) and fat you eat, and increase the percentage of carbohydrate. Fill up on meals of pasta, rice, potato and bread with carb-rich snacks. Carb loading doesn't mean you need to eat more food than normal - you need to try to increase the percentage of carbohydrate in your diet, not the total volume.

3 days before - continue to carb load and keep drinking plenty of fluid, such as water, sports drinks and diluted squash. Add a little salt to your diet at this stage as well. You may notice a bit of weight gain, but this is usually water and stored glycogen, not fat, and to be expected.

2 days before - avoid high-fibre foods such as bran or lots of fruit and don't try anything new.

The night before - have a high-carb meal of pasta, pizza or rice of around 800-1000kcals. Stick with tried-and-tested foods your body is familiar with.

The Ultimate Guide to Marathon Running

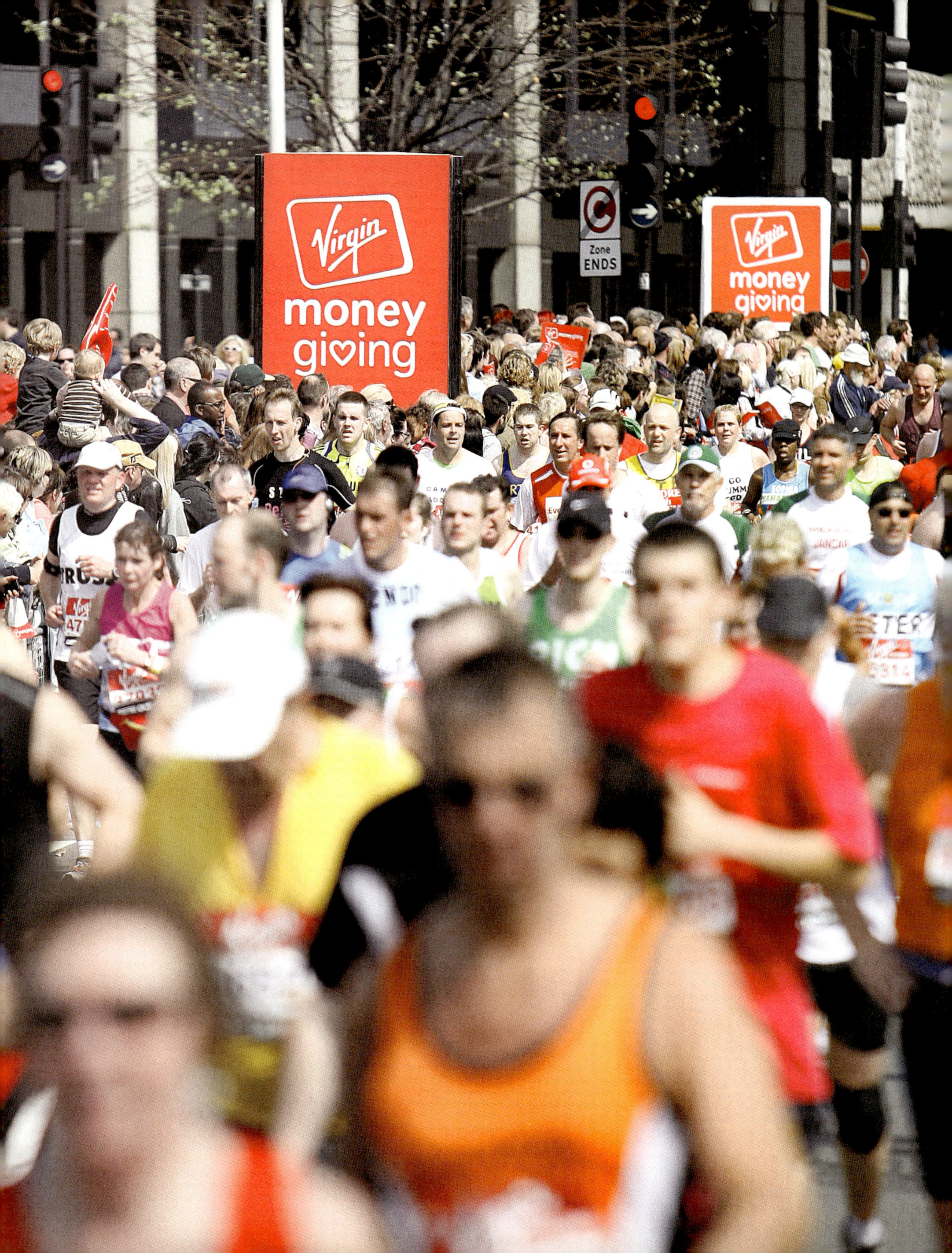
Virgin
money
giving
Zone
ENDS
Virgin
money
giving

Running for charity

■ Thanks to www.realbuzzrunbritain.com for helping to prepare this section

What is charity running all about?

Running a race for charity can be a hugely rewarding activity, allowing you to prove your fitness while raising vital funds for a great cause. There are many different types of charity to run for and numerous ways of getting involved with charity running.

So, what is charity running all about? Is it just a case of raising an agreed amount of money? Well, no. Runners choose to join one particular charity over another for a number of reasons and it is vital that charities maintain a competitive edge by providing more and more for their runners each year. This has given those who take part a real choice because charities offer very contrasting packages.

Not only do runners have a choice of who they run for, they also have a wide choice of where they run and over what distance they eventually run. It's this choice that can make charity running quite confusing for the newcomer.

But don't get overwhelmed by it all. Running for charity is one of the most rewarding experiences you can have and passing that finishing line will, undoubtedly, be one of the highlights of your life.

The feel-good factor of succeeding in a personal challenge while supporting a shared good cause will be felt by all of the race runners.

Why choose to run for charity?

If you have made the decision to run the marathon, why not go the metaphorical extra mile and raise some funds for charity as you go? You may enjoy the running challenge itself, but there is also a wonderful sense of achievement to be had through fundraising.

The past few years have seen a huge increase in charity runners and some charities rely on this fundraising to produce a sizeable proportion of their income. Whether you opt to secure your place through the charity - or you secure your own place and then choose to use it to run on behalf of your chosen charity - it all adds up to much-needed funds.

Top 10 reasons to run for charity

1. You can save the charity money
2. It gives you a purpose for training
3. It gives you motivation for running
4. You may have a personal reason to support a particular charity
5. It can provide a support network for your marathon training
6. Being part of the charity camaraderie on race day
7. Spectator support on race day
8. Gift aid - raise extra funds
9. Raise awareness of the charity you support
10. It's easy to do

Charity fundraising through running

Places in some of the biggest marathon events cost charities money and it is, of course, in their interest to maximise the revenue from each and every place they secure. So it's unfair to commit to run for a charity if you have no real intention of raising the required fundraising target.

For some races, if the charity provides you with an entry, you may be expected to raise as much as £2,000. While that is a major undertaking, it is certainly not impossible. Lots of people have done it before you and had fun in the process.

Many people are put off by the amount that has to be raised, but they shouldn't be. Starting early and getting family and friends on board can take the worry out of fundraising, allowing you to concentrate on your training.

If you have your own place in an event, you can opt to run for a charity and the minimum amount to be raised doesn't apply to you. Anything you raise will be an added bonus for the organisation.

Motivation to run

For many runners, running in memory of a family member, to support a friend or because of their own experience can be the prime motivation for running. What better reason is there to commit to get fit for your running challenge?

With a charity and its cause relying on you, there's less chance of you slacking off on the training and much more chance of you making it to the start - and reaching the finish line.

Support from the charities

Whether it's a 3k fun run or a full marathon, it is vital that charities provide as much practical advice and support as possible to ensure that every runner genuinely feels part of their chosen charity's team.

Training for an event, especially a marathon, requires a huge amount of dedication and the charities will often be on hand with a range of support, from comprehensive training advice and fundraising and sponsorship packs to press targeting. At the actual event, they may provide a pre-race pasta party and post-race massage, so that their runners get the most out of their marathon experience.

Runners will usually receive exclusive team kit and be cheered around the course by the charity's cheerers. You'll be surprised how much of a difference it makes to getting you moving when the mind is willing but the body is unable.

RACE DAY

Race-Day Fuelling

THERE ARE now so many sports-nutrition products on the market that the decision about what to use in the marathon can be confusing. Drinks and gels are probably the best choice because many runners can't tolerate solid food or sports bars while actually running. Sweets such as jelly babies or jelly beans are also a good choice and are often offered in big city marathons – sometimes by spectators holding large bowls full.

The official drink that's provided on the course at your marathon may, eventually, be the deciding factor in what you use, so try to find out what it will be and train with it in advance.

Hopefully, you will have tried various drinks and gels in training, so will know what works best for you. If you are going to use a drink that is not provided on the marathon course, you need to work out a way of carrying it. Try using a Camelbak (so long as you've practised with one) or carrying a bottle that you throw away later. As for gels, pin them to your shorts or shirt, tuck them in your shorts waistband or use a bum-bag to carry them in.

How much carbohydrate do I need?

Leading sports dietician Jane Griffin recommends that 'marathon runners should aim to take in 30-60g of carbohydrate per hour'. This equates to one or two gel packs or about 500-1000ml of sports drink per hour. An average gel contains about 30g of carbohydrate, but check your own brand because they can vary. Your stomach can only absorb a certain amount of carbohydrate during exercise, especially if you're working hard, so if you overdo the gels and drinks, you could end up feeling nauseous – or worse. The 'rule of thumb' of 30-60g may well be too much for you. Experiment with what works best for you. Test it out in training or races and put together a personalised nutrition plan for race day.

TOP TIP: Watch out for the 'water station' signs and swallow your gel just before you get to the next one. Then grab a drink and wash it down with a couple of good mouthfuls of water.

RACE-DAY NUTRITION PLAN

Start taking your gels and sports drinks long before you think you need them. One of the biggest mistakes new marathon runners make is to wait until they feel fatigued at halfway and then start taking carbohydrate on board – by then, it's too late. Your goal is to pre-empt carbohydrate depletion by keeping your levels topped up from the start.

You need to work out a personal nutrition plan for your race, but it could go something like this:

10 minutes before the start – 1 gel washed down with a cup of water

3 miles – 200-300ml sports drink (take sips, don't gulp)

6 miles – 1 gel washed down with a glug of water

10 miles – 200-300ml sports drink

13 miles – 1 gel washed down with glug of water

17 miles – 200-300ml sports drink

20 miles – jelly babies or jelly beans

22 miles – sports drink or water

24 miles – 1 gel washed down with a glug of water

TOP TIP: If the race provides drinks in cups rather than bottles, try to practise drinking on the run beforehand. Pinch the cup into a 'spout', which makes it easier to drink from, and slow right down at water stations. The time spent in slowing down or walking to take a drink is well worth it. Getting severely dehydrated could slow you down a lot more later on or even cause a DNF (did not finish).

The Ultimate Guide to Marathon Running

RACE DAY COMETH

It's finally here: the day you've been waiting and planning for all those months. The bottom line is, try to enjoy it. Here are some things to think about to help ease you through the experience

Waking up
Wake up early (this is almost a given). There are a few exceptions, but most marathons take place first thing in the morning. Wake up early enough to get everything done that needs doing. You are going to need enough time to digest your breakfast before your race: you could try experimenting with this in training.

Have a drink
Try to drink a reasonable amount of liquid when you first wake up and then only sip in the hour leading up to the race to prevent you from needing to make time-consuming bathroom stops along the route.

Eat breakfast
You're going to need something to fuel you round the course. The best advice is to stick to what works for you, but, ideally, this will be a carbohydrate-based breakfast, such as toast, cereal or porridge, eaten in plenty of time to allow your body the necessary time to digest it.

Go to the loo
Use the toilet before you leave home. It's easier said than done, especially at some unholy hour of the morning, but it's better to go at home than try to suffer the inevitable 'queue for the loo' at the race start.

Get there early
Unless the weather is absolutely atrocious and you will not be able to find shelter at the start line, you should try to get to the race early. It will be easier to drop things at the baggage bus, warm up and use the toilets before the crowds appear.

Liaise with the team
If you have friends and family coming to watch and support you, make sure you know where they are. It's not easy to spot loved ones when a) they're among crowds of people b) you're extremely fatigued and c) you don't know where they are!

Finish Finish Finish
Don't put pressure on yourself to achieve a really fast time if it's your first race. Finishing the race and enjoying the experience are excellent goals for a first-timer. Equally, you may feel you need to adjust your goal while you're running (see Tactics and Pacing for more advice).

TOP TIP: If people are coming to watch you, make sure they take a brightly-coloured golfing umbrella and stand in a pre-arranged location. It might sound silly, but it's a lot easier to spot in a crowd.

Marathoning is like cutting yourself unexpectedly. You dip into the pain so gradually that the damage is done before you are aware of it. Unfortunately, when awareness comes, it is excruciating **John Farrington, Australian marathoner**

MARATHON TACTICS
Knowing how you're going to run your marathon is crucial, whether you want to set a personal best or whether you just want to finish. A crude analogy might be the tale of the tortoise and the hare: who got to the finish first in that race? A marathon is a long race: if it were easy, everyone would have done one. It's tough, physically and mentally, but if you know what tactics to adopt, your job might be that bit easier!

The Ultimate Guide to Marathon Running

● RACE **DAY**

THE START

SOME RACES, such as the London Marathon, have multiple starts to cope with the huge numbers of runners in the field. This is not something to be worried about – you won't end up running further, nor will you be crushed when the various starts merge together (although the road does get busier when they do). However, it's probably worth bearing in mind that there's no guarantees you'll be on the same start line as your training partner, friend or family member. Generally, when you're on the start line, you're on your own. This is no bad thing: it gives you time to gather your thoughts and reflect on the challenge you're about to undertake. You'll probably feel the nervous energy in the air – and in yourself – and you can use this to your advantage. But – and I repeat BUT – don't get carried away at the start: you will pay for it later, of that there's no doubt. Most, if not all, marathon races have some sort of seeding at the start: faster runners to the front, slower runners to the back. But given that most application forms ask you to predict a time up to a year before you're due to run, you may find that you're with people who are considerably slower than yourself. This can be a problem, not least because you'll spend the first mile trying to run through the crowds before the field thins out. Don't worry: a more cautious start will probably work in your favour, particularly if it's your first marathon.

If you find yourself among slower runners at the start, don't bob and weave through the crowds or jump up and down kerbs: this wastes precious energy that you'll need in the closing stages of the race.

The Ultimate Guide to Marathon Running

THE FIRST 10 MILES

If you have trained well and are healthy, the first five to 10 miles should seem very easy to you. It might give you an opportunity to talk to some of the other runners around you. You can use this part of the race to establish your rhythm or race-pace and focus on being as relaxed as possible. Renowned endurance coach Bud Baldaro's says: 'You want to feel like you haven't run 10 miles. Whatever pace you think you want to run at, run slower. Getting through this part of the race as easily as possible can be crucial in preserving your energy for when the going gets tough.'

THE SECOND 10 MILES

Somewhere in the second ten miles, runners start to get more serious about the marathon. You'll be less likely to feel like talking and more likely to be focusing on your target splits or on not expending too much energy. You'll stop noticing the landmarks or start appreciating the cheers of the crowd. This is the time the physical and mental simulation you practised before the race will pay off: many people set themselves a 20-mile target time, knowing they've 'only' got six miles left.

THE LAST 6 MILES

This is by far the hardest part of any marathon, although, if you've prepared properly and hydrated along the way, you will be able to get through. There's no denying it will be painful: you will feel fatigue, muscle tightness and soreness during this stage of the race. You'll probably start to experience mental highs and lows: telling yourself you can do it will help see you through.

Somewhere during the last six miles, you will realise that you are going to finish. For many people, this might only be in the last half mile, but it generally provides such a huge psychological lift that you'll barely feel the pain of the final metres (at least, not until you've crossed the finish line!). The last six miles is all about concentration: you've put in the hard work; you can do it.

Get the pace right

The number-one factor in running a successful marathon is the ability to pace yourself. Here are some top tips to see you through that finish line

■ Have a realistic understanding of where you are in your running. This will help you to determine a range of pacing times.
n Be aware that running an even pace is most efficient. The second choice is a negative split (i.e. running the second half of the race quicker than the first half). However, ideal as these might be, most runners tend to slow down in the second half of the race.

■ Learn your numbers. Write your split times on your hand or on a piece of paper tucked into your running shorts if you can't memorise them. Practise race pace in training.

■ Check the race material to learn where split times will be made available. It's generally every mile - or every kilometre, depending on what country you're in.

■ Wear a digital watch or check the clocks along the course. Or, if you really want to know your pace accurately, wear a GPS system: just don't get disheartened if your average split time starts to drop.

■ Be prepared to scale back your pacing plan if the weather is windy or hot - even more so if it is hot and humid. Don't expect to run the same pace if the sun is scorching hot.

■ Try to err on the side of going too slow rather than too fast, particularly in the early stages of the race. You can always make up the time in the later miles, particularly if you've conserved energy.

The Ultimate Guide to Marathon Running

CROSSING THE LINE!

10

steps to the perfect recovery

01 Stop your watch... you have made it! Once you cross that finish line, you have done something that 95% of the population will never achieve. You are a marathon finisher! Never again? That's what everyone says.

02 Soak up the atmosphere around you on the finish line and be proud of your achievement. You're likely to feel incredibly emotional, possibly cry on the shoulder of a complete stranger or feel ecstatic and completely high on adrenaline. Either way, your legs will feel a bit wobbly. One of the most endearing moments of a marathon is in the finish chute, where total strangers wobble and clutch at each other on Bambi-like legs.

03 Take it very easy at this point, walk slowly to the end of the chute to collect your bag and make sure to ask for help if you don't feel well, that's what the medical staff are there for. There should be a team of people to remove your timing chip, so you don't need to bend down to do it.

04 Put your medal around your neck and wear it with pride. Grab a finish poncho or silver blanket and put it on, even if you don't think you need it. After such an endurance effort, your body temperature will drop quickly and it could be a while before you get your bag back.

05 Once you've collected your goodie bag and t-shirt, and retrieved your kit bag, put on some warm clothes, meet up with your family and support team and start to think about refuelling.

06 Even if you feel nauseous, which many marathon finishers do, try to force yourself to eat and drink something. You will be dehydrated and completely depleted of all carbohydrate. Refuelling within the first 20 minutes or so of crossing the line is the most important thing you can do to help your recovery.
Eat anything you can stomach from your goodie bag, have a sports drink or milkshake and try to include some salt in the form of an electrolyte drink, salty crisps or even chips!

07 Do not even consider stretching at this point. Your muscles will be damaged with millions of micro-tears and stretching them immediately after the marathon can make matters worse. Keep walking around and try some very gentle stretches later, when you get home.

08 The jury is still out on ice baths, but many runners swear by them on the basis that ice therapy speeds up recovery. If you want to try it, fill your bath with ice cold water, about 12-inches deep. Wear a warm sweatshirt and aim to sit in it for about 10 minutes. Alternatively try running ice-cold water on your legs in the shower, alternating with warm.

09 Book in for a very gentle massage the next day. This will help flush the lactic acid from your muscles and promote faster recovery. Make sure your therapist is well qualified in sports massage and tell them that you have just completed a marathon - although the way you walk into their therapy room might give the game away.

10 There's only one thing left to do... celebrate! Even if you didn't quite hit your target time or things didn't go exactly to plan, still be proud of what you achieved. You are a marathon runner and not many people can stake claim to that.... Cheers!

FAST FACT

The last person in the 2009 Flora London Marathon finished in 8hrs 50mins and 21secs

Post-marathon days

IN THE days after the marathon, you will likely feel very tired, very stiff and mentally exhausted. The soreness in your legs is because of millions of micro-tears in the cells of your muscles – known as DOMS (Delayed Onset Muscle Soreness) – and usually peaks at 48-72 hours after the race. It's also perfectly normal to get post-marathon blues and feel a bit 'down'. After the nervous build up, the excitement, adrenaline and post-race exhaustion, it's hardly surprising.

Take the time now to get plenty of sleep, eat well and rest as much as you can, which will help mentally as well as physically. Remember to drink lots of water and spend some time walking and stretching. You could even indulge in some light exercise – just make sure it's not running!

Revel in this post-marathon glory, tell anyone who will listen all about it and give your body and mind time to recover before you rush back into training or start planning your next event or challenge.

REVERSE TAPER

Many runners describe the post-marathon recovery process as a 'reverse taper'. How quickly you recover will depend on your fitness level going into the race, how hard you pushed it in the marathon and how long you've been running. The general rule of thumb, however, is that full recovery from a marathon effort takes approximately three to four weeks.

Go for a walk on Monday and Tuesday, and perhaps by Thursday you may feel up to a very, very gentle run. Start at a very slow pace and just jog out for about three miles or so. No long runs and absolutely no speed-work. You could try a little cross-training – a swim or a spin on the bike are both ideal.

After about seven to 10 days, you should be ready to ease back into some normal-pace runs and to pick up your training again. But take it easy and, if you feel unusually tired or have any niggles, back off and rest some more. You should be fully recovered after approximately three to four weeks and ready to get back into training – and even some racing.

Use your marathon endurance and have a go at some 10k and half-marathon events or even mix things up with some cross-training and have a crack at a triathlon. Most races will now seem blissfully short in comparison. Equally, you might decide that you want to just enjoy your running for a while. Whatever you choose, you know you'll have your marathon finish behind you.

WHAT NEXT?

If you're anything like most marathon runners, the temptation of seeing if you can go faster next time will be too hard to resist. If you want to enter another marathon, give yourself at least four to six months to recover and rebuild before you race the distance again. Take stock of what went well and what didn't. Learn from your successes and mistakes, write it all down and take heed as you start your marathon journey all over again... but never forget your amazing achievement. YOU are a marathon runner. Congratulations!

The Ultimate Guide to Marathon Running

Schedules

TRAINING SCHEDULES

By the time you start these schedules, you should already have laid down a valuable training base for your marathon, no matter what time you're expecting to run

With roughly 12 weeks to go before the big day, these schedules are designed to try to inject some mid-programme quality and enthusiasm into your training. Although we've split the schedules into various target times, we expect anyone attempting any of these schedules not to jump into them feet first without having done at least a month's worth of steady running. Hopefully, these schedules will add some variety and quality to your training to shave minutes off your predicted time.

The Ultimate Guide to Marathon Running

● 4HRS PLUS
or get me round in one piece

WEEK 1

Friday	3 miles	Easy run or rest if you want to
Saturday	Hills	Jog two miles easy to a hill you know. Then run five or six times up it and recover jogging down
Sunday	7-8 miles	Run as you feel, anything between 10-12mins/mile
Monday	Rest	After that weekend, you've earned it
Tuesday	5 miles	Steady run, try to up the pace a bit
Wednesday	Rest or swim	
Thursday	3 miles	Steady run

WEEK 2

Friday	Rest	
Saturday	Session	Try to get your body used to running that little bit faster than your normal pace. Jog two miles as an easy warm-up and then run six repetitions of 60 secs with a couple of minutes' walk between each. Jog back home
Sunday	9 miles	Almost double figures
Monday	Rest	
Tuesday	5 miles	Easy run. How are your legs after the weekend?
Wednesday	Rest or swim	
Thursday	6 miles	Steady run, slightly faster than race pace

WEEK 3

Friday	3 miles	Easy run or optional rest day
Saturday	Rest	
Sunday	**RACE**	Try to find a 10k or 10-mile race this weekend. It could be a good opportunity to see what sort of shape you're in
Monday	Rest	
Tuesday	5 miles	Easy run
Wednesday	Rest or swim	
Thursday	8 miles	Steady pace

Any schedule is only designed to be a guide to your marathon training. Of course, you could follow it religiously. But it's up to you to adapt it as you go along.

WEEK 4

Friday	Rest	
Saturday	5 miles	Easy run
Sunday	11 miles	Your longest run so far. Take it easy and aim to complete
Monday	Rest	
Tuesday	4 miles	Run as you feel
Wednesday	Rest	
Thursday	Session	6 x 1min with 2mins recovery between reps. Do a two-mile easy warm-up and then aim to run the reps faster than race pace. Jog back home
Friday	Rest	

The Ultimate Guide to Marathon Running

● 4HRS PLUS
or get me round in one piece

WEEK 5

Friday	3 miles	Easy run or rest if you want to
Saturday	Hills	Jog two miles easy to a hill you know. Then run five or six times up it and recover jogging down
Sunday	10 miles	Run as you feel, anything between 10-12mins/mile
Monday	Rest	After that weekend, you've earned it
Tuesday	5 miles	Steady run, try to up the pace a bit
Wednesday	Rest or swim	
Thursday	3 miles	Steady run

WEEK 6

Friday	Rest	
Saturday	Session	Jog two miles as an easy warm-up and then run six repetitions of 2mins with a couple of minutes' walk between each. Jog back home
Sunday	13 miles	This is half the distance of the actual event! Aim to run this slowly: your goal is to finish feeling like you could have carried on
Monday	Rest	
Tuesday	5 miles	Easy run. How are your legs after the weekend?
Wednesday	Rest or swim	
Thursday	8 miles	Steady run, slightly faster than race pace

WEEK 7

Friday	3 miles	Easy run or optional rest day
Saturday	Rest	
Sunday	**RACE**	Try to find a half-marathon race this weekend. It could be a good opportunity to see what sort of shape you're in
Monday	Rest	
Tuesday	5 miles	Easy run
Wednesday	Rest or swim	
Thursday	8 miles	Steady pace

> If you're ill, take a rest day. If you feel overly tired, take a rest day. If the kids are getting you down, take a rest day. Don't be afraid of rest!

WEEK 8

Friday	Rest	
Saturday	5 miles	Easy run
Sunday	15 miles	Your longest run so far. Take it easy and aim to complete
Monday	Rest	
Tuesday	4 miles	Run as you feel
Wednesday	Rest	
Thursday	Session	6 x 3mins with 2mins recovery between reps. Do a two-mile easy warm-up and then aim to run the reps faster than race pace. Jog back home
Friday	Rest	

The Ultimate Guide to Marathon Running

● 4HRS PLUS
or get me round in one piece

WEEK 9

Friday	3 miles	Easy run or rest if you want to
Saturday	Rest	
Sunday	**RACE**	My advice would be to do a half and not a 20-miler (too close to race distance and possibility of injury). It's the last real opportunity before you begin a gradual taper
Monday	Rest	If you're anything like me, your legs will be sore, so take it easy
Tuesday	5 miles	Steady run - your legs may still be feeling the effects
Wednesday	Rest or swim	
Thursday	3 miles	Steady run

WEEK 10

Friday	Rest	
Saturday	Session	No reason why you can't do a session today. Aim for something like 90secs reps with an easy 2mins jog recovery. Run them faster than race pace
Sunday	Long run	Aim for 2-2hrs 30mins, but no more. Why get injured now?
Monday	Rest	
Tuesday	5 miles	Easy run. How are your legs after the weekend?
Wednesday	Rest or swim	
Thursday	8 miles	Steady run, slightly faster than race pace

WEEK 11

Friday	3 miles	Easy run or optional rest day
Saturday	Rest	
Sunday	**RACE** or session	If there's a 10k you fancy, I see no reason why you shouldn't have a go. If not, try a steady-paced run with a few faster efforts: aim for six miles in total
Monday	Rest	
Tuesday	5 miles	Easy run
Wednesday	Rest or swim	
Thursday	6 miles	Steady pace

FINAL WEEK

Friday	Rest	
Saturday	5 miles	Easy run
Sunday	8 miles	The last longer run. Take it easy: one week to go!
Monday		Rest
Tuesday	4 miles	Run as you feel
Wednesday	Rest	
Thursday	3 miles	Very easy run, with a few small efforts
Friday	Rest	
Saturday	Gentle jog	
Sunday	**MARATHON RACE**	

The Ultimate Guide to Marathon Running

● 3HRS 30MINS
The marathon virgin – seasoned runner or optimistic beginner

WEEK 1

Friday	Rest	
Saturday	Session	Two sets (3mins hard, 2mins rest, 2mins hard) with 2mins rest between sets
Sunday	12 miles	Run as you feel, slow to medium pace
Monday	5 miles	Listen to your body and run as you feel
Tuesday	Session	6 x 3mins at threshold pace with 60secs between reps
Wednesday	5 miles	Steady run, try to up the pace a bit
Thursday	6 miles	Steady run

WEEK 2

Friday	Rest	
Saturday	**RACE**	Cross country or 10k or 6-mile tempo run
Sunday	13 miles	Easy, slow pace
Monday	5 miles	Easy run
Tuesday	Hills	Two-mile easy warm-up and then 8 hill reps of around 60secs with a jog back recovery
Wednesday	5 miles	Steady run
Thursday	6 miles	Tempo run; try to run two 10-minute efforts at slightly faster than race pace

WEEK 3

Friday	Rest	
Saturday	3 miles	Easy run
Sunday	RACE	Try to find a half-marathon race this weekend. It could be a good opportunity to see what sort of shape you're in
Monday	Rest	Or optional recovery run if you want to stretch those legs
Tuesday	6 miles	Easy run
Wednesday	7 miles	Steady run
Thursday	Session	4 x 4mins at threshold pace with 60-90secs between reps

WEEK 4

Friday	Rest	
Saturday	5 miles	Steady run
Sunday	14 miles	Easy run – get used to the time on your feet
Monday	5 miles	Easy run
Tuesday	Hills	Two-mile easy warm-up and then 8 hill reps of around 60secs with a jog back recovery
Wednesday	5 miles	Steady run
Thursday	5 miles	Steady run

The Ultimate Guide to Marathon Running

● 3HRS 30MINS
The marathon virgin – seasoned runner or optimistic beginner

WEEK 5

Friday	Rest	
Saturday	Session	Three sets (4mins hard, 2mins rest, 2mins hard) with 2mins rest between sets
Sunday	15 miles	Run as you feel, slow to medium pace
Monday	5 miles	Listen to your body and run as you feel
Tuesday	Session	6 x 3mins at threshold pace with 60secs between reps
Wednesday	5 miles	Steady run
Thursday	8 miles	Steady run

WEEK 6

Friday	Rest	
Saturday	Session	Three sets 4mins hard, 2mins rest, 2mins hard) with 2mins rest between sets
Sunday	15 miles	Run as you feel, slow to medium pace
Monday	5 miles	Listen to your body and run as you feel
Tuesday	Session	6 x 3mins at threshold pace with 60secs between reps
Wednesday	5 miles	Steady run
Thursday	8 miles	Tempo run; try to run two 10-minute efforts at slightly faster than race pace

WEEK 7

Friday	Rest	
Saturday	3 miles	Easy run
Sunday	**RACE**	Try to find a half-marathon race this weekend. It could be a good opportunity to see what sort of shape you're in
Monday	Rest	Or optional recovery run if you want to stretch those legs
Tuesday	6 miles	Easy run
Wednesday	7 miles	Steady run
Thursday	Session	4 x 5mins at threshold pace with 60-90secs between reps

WEEK 8

Friday	Rest	
Saturday	5 miles	Steady run
Sunday	19-20 miles	Easy run – get used to the time on your feet
Monday	5 miles	Easy run
Tuesday	Hills	Two-mile easy warm-up and then 8 hill reps of around 60secs with a jog back recovery
Wednesday	5 miles	Steady run
Thursday	8 miles	Tempo run, with at least 30mins at a strong pace

The Ultimate Guide to Marathon Running

158

3HRS 30MINS
The marathon virgin – seasoned runner or optimistic beginner

WEEK 9

Friday	Steady	5 miles
Saturday	Rest	
Sunday	**RACE**	My advice would be to do a half not a 20-miler (too close to race distance and possibility of injury). It's the last real opportunity before you begin a gradual taper. If you run a PB, it will be a great confidence booster
Monday	5 miles	Or rest if legs sore
Tuesday	Session	7 x 3mins at threshold pace, with 60 secs between reps
Wednesday	5 miles	Easy run
Thursday	8 miles	Tempo run: take a mile to warm up, then run 30 minutes at race pace or faster, with a mile or so easy warm down

WEEK 10

Friday	Rest	
Saturday	6 miles	Steady run
Sunday	20 miles	The last big run. Aim for up to 2hrs 30mins, but no more
Monday	5 miles	Easy run
Tuesday	Hills	Two-mile easy warm-up and then 9 hill reps of around 60secs with a jog back recovery
Wednesday	5 miles	Easy run or rest
Thursday	8 miles	Tempo run; try to run two 15-minute efforts at slightly faster than race pace

WEEK 11

Friday	Rest	
Saturday	3 miles	Easy run
Sunday	14 miles	Cutting the distance now will help prevent injury
Monday	Rest	Or optional recovery run if you want to stretch those legs
Tuesday	6 miles	Easy run
Wednesday	7 miles	Steady run
Thursday	Session	4 x 3mins at threshold pace with 60-90secs between reps

FINAL WEEK

Friday	Rest	
Saturday	5 miles	Steady run
Sunday	10 miles	Easy run – just a last, longish, slow run
Monday	5 miles	Easy run
Tuesday	3 miles	Easy
Wednesday	3 miles	Put in two or three efforts, but don't overdo it
Thursday	Rest	
Friday	Rest	
Saturday	Gentle jog	
Sunday	**MARATHON RACE**	

The final week is your taper week. Make sure you reduce your mileage, but try to keep a little of the quality, e.g. throw in a couple of 60-second reps.

The Ultimate Guide to Marathon Running

● SUB 2HRS 55MINS
PB hunter – club runner

WEEK 1

Friday	7 miles easy	
Saturday	Race or pyramid session	2 x (4mins, 3mins, 2mins, 1min) with 60secs recovery between reps and four minutes easy jog between sets
Sunday	14 miles	Easy run, 7-7.30min/mile
Monday	5-7 miles	Easy/steady run
Tuesday	7 miles	Steady run
Wednesday	5 miles	Easy/steady run
Thursday	8 miles sub-6min/mile	Try to put 30 minutes of tempo running into this session,

WEEK 2

Friday	Rest	
Saturday	Session	6-7 x 3mins at threshold pace
Sunday	15 miles	You should be looking to cover at least 2hrs in your long run at this point. Given that it takes three weeks to feel the effect of any training session, now's the time to put in the miles – as well as keep on top of the quality
Monday	6 miles	Easy run, as you feel
Tuesday	Hills	Warm up with a two-mile jog. Find a hill that will take between 60-80secs of hard running to complete and then do 8-12 repetitions. Jog back home
Wednesday	6 miles	Easy run
Thursday	7 miles	Tempo run, looking to run at race pace or slightly faster

WEEK 3

Friday	Rest	
Saturday	5 miles	Easy if racing tomorrow
Sunday	**RACE**	Try to find a half-marathon race this weekend. It could be a good opportunity to see what sort of shape you're in
Monday	5 miles	Easy recovery run
Tuesday	Session	5 x 5mins with 90secs recovery at threshold pace
Wednesday	5 miles	Medium pace
Thursday	10 miles	Aim to run 40 minutes at tempo pace (i.e. sub-6min/mile)

WEEK 4

Friday	Rest	
Saturday	Hills	Warm up with a two-mile jog. Find a hill that will take between 60-80secs of hard running to complete and then do 10-12 repetitions. Jog back home
Sunday	16 miles	Slow, chatting pace
Monday	8 miles	Run as you feel
Tuesday	Session	4 x 60secs, 4 x 2mins, 2 x 4mins, 4 x 2mins (take 60secs between reps and 2-2.30 mins between sets)
Wednesday	6 miles	Easy run
Thursday	10 miles	Run 45 minutes of this at tempo pace

The Ultimate Guide to Marathon Running

● SUB 2HRS 55MINS
PB hunter – club runner

WEEK 5

Friday	7 miles easy	
Saturday	Race or pyramid session	2 x (5mins, 4mins, 3mins, 2mins, 1min) with 60secs recovery between reps and four minutes easy jog between sets
Sunday	16 miles	Easy run, 7-7.30min/mile
Monday	5-7 miles	Easy/steady run
Tuesday	7 miles	Steady run
Wednesday	5 miles	Easy/steady run
Thursday	8 miles sub-6min/mile	Try to put 30 minutes of tempo running into this session,

WEEK 6

Friday	Rest	
Saturday	Session	7-9 x 3mins at threshold pace
Sunday	18 miles	You should be looking to cover at least 2hrs in your long run at this point. Given that it takes three weeks to feel the effect of any training session, now's the time to put in the miles
Monday	8 miles	Easy run, as you feel
Tuesday	Hills	Warm up with a two-mile jog. Find a hill that will take between 60-80secs of hard running to complete and then do 8-12 repetitions. Jog back home
Wednesday	6 miles	Easy run
Thursday	9 miles	Tempo run, looking to run at race pace or slightly faster

WEEK 7

Friday	Rest	
Saturday	5 miles	Easy if racing tomorrow
Sunday	**RACE**	Try to find a half-marathon race this weekend. It could be a good opportunity to see what sort of shape you're in
Monday	5 miles	Easy recovery run
Tuesday	Session	5-6 x 5mins with 90secs recovery at threshold pace
Wednesday	5 miles	Medium pace
Thursday	10 miles	Aim to run 40 minutes of this at tempo pace (i.e. sub-6minutes/mile)

WEEK 8

Friday	Rest	
Saturday	Hills	Warm up with a two-mile jog. Find a hill that will take between 60-80secs of hard running to complete and then do 10-12 repetitions. Jog back home
Sunday	20 miles	Slow, chatting pace
Monday	8 miles	Run as you feel
Tuesday	Session	4 x 60 secs, 4 x 2mins, 2 x 4mins, 4 x 2mins (take 60secs between reps and 2-2.30 minutes between sets
Wednesday	6 miles	Easy run
Thursday	10 miles	Run 45 minutes of this at tempo pace

The Ultimate Guide to Marathon Running

● SUB 2HRS 55MINS
PB hunter – club runner

WEEK 9

Friday	7 miles easy	
Saturday	Race or pyramid session	2 x (5mins, 4mins, 3mins, 2mins, 1min) with 60secs recovery between reps and four minutes easy jog between sets
Sunday	20 miles	Easy run, 7-7.30min/mile
Monday	5 miles	Easy/steady run
Tuesday	Session	6 x 1 mile with a minute's recovery
Wednesday	Rest	
Thursday	8 miles sub-6min/mile	Try to put 30 minutes of tempo running into this session,

WEEK 10

Friday	Rest	
Saturday	RACE	Or session. Could be the last hard outing before the big day. If racing, opt for a competitive half or, if not, 7-9 x 3mins at threshold pace
Sunday	17 miles	Last longish run
Monday	8 miles	Easy run, as you feel
Tuesday	Hills	Warm up with a two-mile jog. Find a hill that will take 60-80secs of hard running to complete and do 10 reps
Wednesday	6 miles	Easy run
Thursday	6 miles	Tempo run, looking to run at race pace or slightly faster

WEEK 11

Friday	Rest	
Saturday	5 miles	Easy if racing tomorrow
Sunday	75 mins	
Monday	5 miles	Easy recovery run
Tuesday	Session	4 x 5mins with 90secs recovery at threshold pace
Thursday	5 miles	Medium pace
Thursday	6 miles	Tempo run, but as you feel

FINAL WEEK

Friday	Rest	
Saturday	5 miles	Steady
Sunday	9 miles	Very slow
Monday	4 miles	Run as you feel
Tuesday	4 miles	Do 4 x 60secs light efforts
Wednesday	REST	
Thursday	3 miles	
Friday	REST	
Saturday	Gentle jog	
Sunday	**MARATHON RACE**	

Make sure you have a race strategy in mind. Know your splits, write them on your wrist or use a pacing band. And don't go off too fast – you'll pay for it later!

The Ultimate Guide to Marathon Running